Family Message Journals

Family Message Journals

Teaching Writing through Family Involvement

Julie E. Wollman-Bonilla
Rhode Island College

National Council of Teachers of English
1111 W. Kenyon Road, Urbana, Illinois 61801-1096

Staff Editor: Bonny Graham

Interior Design: Doug Burnett

Cover Design: Jenny Jensen Greenleaf

NCTE Stock Number: 52457-3050

Library of Congress Cataloging-in-Publication Data

Wollman-Bonilla, Julie.
     Family message journals: teaching writing through family involvement / Julie E. Wollman-Bonilla.
          p. cm.
     Includes bibliographical references (p.).
     ISBN 0-8141-5245-7 (pbk)
       1. English language—Composition and exercises—Study and teaching (Elementary) 2. Education, Elementary—Parent participation. 3. Language arts (Elementary) I. Title.

     LB1576.W644 2000
     372.62'3044—dc21

                                                                    99-089727

For my family of writers—LuLu, Panda, Pop

Contents

Acknowledgments

I owe deepest thanks to Kristen, Kyle, Maryanne, Sara, and their families for entrusting me with their Family Message Journals. Their work made this book possible and enlivens it with wonderful examples of the possibilities of Family Message Journals. Likewise, this book would not have been possible without Dina Carolan and Karen Wilensky, inspiring teachers who generously shared their ideas and their feedback on the manuscript. It is a pleasure for me to be able to make their fine work accessible to others.

Pete Feely, NCTE K–12 Acquisitions Editor, fielded my questions and concerns with good humor and good advice. He is a thoughtful, calm, and reassuring guide, and a good listener. And thanks to Pat Cordeiro, my colleague at Rhode Island College, for believing in my idea and putting me in touch with Pete.

1 Challenging Assumptions about Learning to Write and Teaching Writing

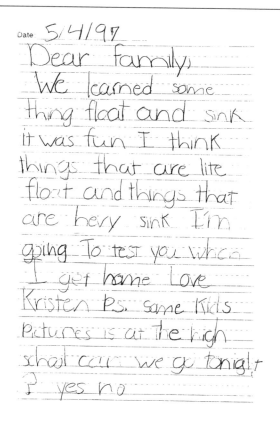

Date: 5/4/97

Dear family,
We learned some
thing float and sink
it was fun I think
things that are lite
float and things that
are hevy sink I'm
going To test you when
I get home Love
Kristen P.s. some Kids
Pictures is at The high
schol can we go tonight
? yes no

5/4/97
Dear Family,
      We learned some things float and sink. It was fun. I think things that are
light float and things that are heavy sink. I'm going to test you when I get home.
Love, Kristen
P.S. Some kids' pictures is at the high school. Can we go tonight?
Yes No

Figure 1.1. Kristen's message allows her to review a subject of study and share her new knowledge with her family.

Kristen wrote the message in Figure 1.1 in her Family Message Journal after she participated in a science experiment in her first-grade classroom. Before the experiment, students were asked to hypothesize which of the objects the teacher showed them might float and which might sink. Then, in small groups the children tested their hypotheses with a bucket of water and a collection of objects. Next, they were asked to explain their findings: Why do certain things sink and others float? Finally, the first graders were assigned to write about the experiment in their Family Message Journals.

In a brief prewriting discussion, the class considered possibilities for the content of their messages. Guided by the teacher, various students suggested that they might write their original predictions about what would happen, explain how they did the experiment, or tell what they had learned. Kristen used her message to review for herself and share with her family what she had learned. She also wrote that she would test her family members' knowledge of objects' behavior in water when she got home. Thus the message served to inform Kristen's family about a specific school activity and also functioned as a reminder for her family to talk about Kristen's learning later that day, providing another opportunity for informal review and extension of her knowledge.

What Are Family Message Journals?

I was introduced to Family Message Journals by Kristen's first-grade teacher, Dina Carolan, whose ideas, along with those of her colleague Karen Wilensky, were the catalyst for this book. Family Message Journals are notebooks in which children write a message to their families each day about something they did or learned or thought about in school, and a family member (or other willing adult, aside from the classroom teacher) writes a message in reply. Because children's messages are written in school about classroom activities, they *truly* inform family members about something they do not know or about activities in which they did not participate. The concept of Family Message Journals originated with Karen. One of *her* son's elementary teachers had students write messages every Friday, telling their families what they had done in school that week. This gave Karen the idea for a more dialogic form of communication: a journal that included family replies and that was, in her words, "more curriculum-based"—with children's messages structured around daily curriculum activities and larger goals.

Family Message Journals differ from typical primary grade journals in that the messages serve specific learning and communication purposes. The children do not select their own message topics, and they generally do not write about things they know their families already know, such as their weekend experiences or events of the previous evening. Rather, the messages serve as genuine communication of ideas, knowledge, and needs unknown to family members. The messages are about what children learned that day in specific curriculum areas (e.g., art, health, language arts, mathematics, reading, social studies, or science), or they inform families about school events and necessities, such as bringing a bag lunch for a field trip.

Why Use Family Message Journals?

Family Message Journals are relatively simple to initiate and incorporate into existing curricula and classroom routines, yet the simplicity of application should not mask this strategy's many benefits. The journals are a manageable way for teachers to involve families on a daily basis in children's school learning and literacy development, and they are an effective way to provide real purposes and audiences for children's early writing.

Involving Families

Despite good intentions, families are often uncertain about treading on school "territory." They may lack knowledge about how best to help their children in school, and many lack time to become engaged in activities during the school day, but this does not mean they are not genuinely interested. And, although families are usually eager to know what is happening in classrooms, children's typical response to questions about what they did in school is "Nothing." This lack of communication frustrates families, but few feel it is appropriate to "bother" the teacher with questions about daily work. So most families restrain themselves from contacting their children's teachers until they have more pressing concerns.

Teachers, too, are frustrated by the challenge of how to bridge school learning and children's home experiences. They want families to be aware that something *is* happening in school and that they can become partners in classroom learning, but teachers also tend to doubt family willingness or ability to get involved (Baumann & Thomas, 1997; Fact and Fiction, 1997/98; Delgado-Gaitan, 1990; Hoover-Dempsey & Sandler, 1995, 1997).

Kristen's message is an example of how Family Message Journals can begin to address the challenges intrinsic to family involvement. The journals provide daily information about school experiences and can serve as written reminders of activities for children to discuss at home. This discussion and related endeavors support and extend children's learning, as did Kristen's "test" for her family. During the test she again explained (this time orally) why certain things float and others sink. Her family then challenged her to continue learning, as together they considered certain intermediate weight objects not used in the school experiment, helping Kristen refine her understanding of which objects are light enough to float in water.

In other home discussions that were sparked by Family Message Journal entries about this same experiment, other families discussed whether the results might differ if a liquid other than water were used. Such discussions often involve fathers or other males, who (due to social norms) are far less likely than female family members ever to have visited school during the day or volunteered in the classroom. This was certainly the case for the families in the first-grade classrooms highlighted in this book. All parent/guardian volunteers who worked in the classrooms and accompanied the classes on field trips were mothers or grandmothers of the first graders. Family Message Journals reach out to the males in children's homes and involve them in ways that other family involvement activities may not.

Promoting Children's Development as Writers

A second challenge for teachers is how to assist young children's writing development by helping them appreciate what writing can do for them and introducing them to the many forms of writing that may help them accomplish their academic and social goals (Milz, 1985). By requiring her students to write about the science experiment on buoyancy, Dina Carolan introduced her students to a scientific genre, in which hypotheses and, later, empirical findings are recorded. Kristen's message focuses on her original hypothesis about objects' weight determining their buoyancy, which was confirmed through experimentation. Composing it also introduced her to the value of writing as a way to remember plans, in this case her plan to test her family's knowledge of which objects might float and which might sink in water. Additionally, this message helped Kristen see how writing can be a tool for reviewing what was learned—putting it into her own words and having it to look back at as a memory aid.

Kristen also took advantage of the Family Message Journal to accomplish a purely social purpose—requesting that her family attend the townwide student art show at the high school. She even created a forced choice, asking her family to answer her by circling "yes" or "no" on her journal entry. This common technique in the first graders' journals passed from one student to another throughout the year; they discovered they were more likely to get direct answers to specific requests by forcing families to choose one of two options. Otherwise, family members might respond only to the other content of the message and fail to answer the question.

Family Message Journals were also used to question families about curriculum-related issues. For example, assigned homework projects were often introduced to families through a journal entry in which children were instructed to enlist help, as Sara did:

> 11/1/96
> squeak mom and Dad
> We are learning about mice in our first grade room. I. have.a mouse
> fact to research Will You help me Please?

In this case, it was Sara's father who helped her, using a CD-ROM encyclopedia as well as a few information books Sara had at home. This was involvement he could manage, although he arrived home from work long after school was over and the town library was closed. Writing the reply message was also a way for him to be involved in Sara's school learning:

> 11/1/96
> Dear Sara,
> I really enjoyed helping you learn how to research your home-
> work question. I'm looking forward to working together lots more!
> Love, Papa

Because of his work schedule, the Family Message Journal was the only way for Sara's father to participate in her school learning. And the level of participation invited by the journal went far beyond the usual— simply supervising the completion of homework.

Family Message Journals represent genuine communication between children and their families. Teachers know that the kinds of real purposes and audiences Kristen and Sara enjoyed are essential to maximizing learning and interest in writing. Children pay more attention to communicating fully and clearly in their writing when they know someone is going to read it and be truly informed. But how many "real-world" readers will patiently wade through a first grader's invented spellings on a regular basis? And how many will provide replies frequently enough to reinforce the idea that there is a real audience out there reading a child's work and caring enough about it to respond (and thereby provide feedback on its communicative effectiveness)? A family member is usually willing to do so on a daily basis because families have a commitment to their own children and because reading and answering one message takes only a few minutes each day.

Family Message Journals as a Flexible Strategy

I have argued that the use of Family Message Journals is a strategy that needs to be shared because it begins to address key challenges in teaching writing. The rest of this book will elaborate on how this happens, what the teacher's role is in making it happen, and what teachers who implement this strategy can expect to find in children's Family Message Journals. But first, it is important to note that another aspect of the journals' power as a classroom tool is flexibility.

Because Family Message Journals are an open-ended activity, and because their basic structure is very simple, they are highly adaptable. For example, children who have difficulty with writing may dictate or word process their entries, depending on their specific needs. Some of the first graders' entries collected for this book were word processed, though the great majority were handwritten because of a scarcity of computers in the classrooms.

Family Message Journals are also adaptable to any grade level. It would be unfortunate if the fact that my examples come from grade 1 classrooms implied that Family Message Journals are predominantly a primary grade strategy. Though family involvement tends to be more common in the lower grades, it is important to try to extend this trend because of the many benefits of involving families. As teachers should be able to envision throughout the book, Family Message Journals have the flexibility to be used at any grade level, and their open-ended nature makes them workable for students with diverse abilities and needs within a single classroom. Some children will be expected to write much more than others. Some emergent writers may mix drawing and print early in the year, while others may communicate through drawing alone. Since messages are read at home, the child can help family members make sense of his or her communicative intentions, if necessary.

In the upper grades, children will be able to write longer messages in less time, but the messages can still be linked to curriculum and daily instructional goals. Messages might also be focused on more extended, extensive theme studies, or they might center on independent research projects and be one way for teachers, students, and families to monitor progress. Of course, expectations will also differ at the upper-grade levels with respect to message clarity and length, and the demonstrated depth of involvement and understanding of curriculum topics.

Children whose families speak a language other than English may correspond in their home language or write in English and receive replies in the home language. When they write in English, they sometimes translate into the home language for their families while sharing their messages. Bilingual families are a special resource when using Family Message Journals because they give children opportunities to practice and appreciate their home languages as well as English. The use of more than one language in Family Message Journals also introduces new languages into the classroom, developing every student's awareness of the many ways to communicate and the choices we must make as speakers and writers in light of our audience. Chapter 3 elaborates on the issue of adapting Family Message Journals to children's and families' diverse strengths and needs.

What Can We Learn about Writing Instruction from Family Message Journals?

Family Message Journals are not simply an effective, flexible strategy. They can also teach us something about writing instruction in general. They represent a meeting point between seemingly divergent theories, as well as a way of translating theoretical ideals into sensible, responsible classroom practice. As I will elaborate in the following chapters, Family Message Journals integrate principles of student ownership; frequent, purposeful writing; and regular, genuine response with the recognition that teachers play an important role in guiding children to recognize, appreciate, and appropriate multiple purposes and genres for writing. Teachers can do this through instruction which expands children's knowledge and by assigning topics which challenge children to write about things and in ways they might never choose independently. For example, Kristen's message about the buoyancy experiment is rudimentary scientific writing, organized around recording hypotheses and reporting findings.

What Dina Carolan has done, however, is not wait for children to discover this type of writing on their own. She does not, for example, allow some children to tell a story related to the experiment because they are unfamiliar with scientific writing. Rather, she discusses with her students what types of content and forms belong in different sorts of messages. In short, she moves her students beyond where they might go alone if given free choice of the topics and genres used in their Family Message Journals, and she supports them in trying new ways of writing that they cannot yet accomplish on their own (Applebee & Langer, 1983; Cazden, 1988; Langer & Applebee, 1986; Rogoff & Gardner, 1984; Vygotsky, 1978; Wood, Bruner, & Ross, 1976).

But I did not view Family Message Journals in such a positive light at first, and I suspect my initial reaction may be shared by others. Yes, they get children writing daily, and they include families in their children's school learning, showing that the teacher values family participation. But children were *told* what to write about and often instructed in writing specific types of messages—a scientific observation based on a small-group experiment, a story about the tooth fairy, or a persuasive piece on recycling, for example. I was concerned that this approach was likely to preclude ownership and interest in writing. I wondered: Shouldn't children's writing be self-directed because this helps them discover the value and power of writing? I doubt I am alone in asking this question.

Throughout the last fifteen years of publications on teaching writing, we have been frequently reminded of the importance of choice as the key to ownership and commitment in children's writing (e.g., Calkins, 1986, 1994; Graves, 1983). Although many authors have asserted that teachers' support is important in helping children make the most of their individual writing choices, and some attention to selected genres has been recommended in recent years, the prevailing "wisdom" is that we must not intervene too much or the writing will no longer belong to the children. How many times have we heard teachers ask (or asked ourselves), "I can't tell my students what to write, can I? Doesn't that make the writing mine and not theirs?" Or, "I can't believe this new state writing assessment! The children have to write on an *assigned* topic! How can they do *that* successfully?" We have convinced ourselves that our students cannot write, at least not well, without personal choice of their topics.

And yet, despite our commitment to child-centered writing instruction and individual choice and ownership, many of us worry. Too many elementary classrooms, influenced by the liberating principles of the writing process movement, exhibit a lack of systematic instruction or required activities that teach children how writing functions and what forms it takes in the world and then engage them in applying what they have learned. As a whole, school children in the United States do not seem to be particularly facile with various types of writing as they move through the elementary years and into middle and high school. Most have experienced a steady diet of personal and fictional narrative.

Fortunately, I had the opportunity to visit the first-grade classroom of Dina Carolan once a week from October through May of the 1996–97 school year. There, I observed and facilitated students' writing in their Family Message Journals, among many other activities. Dina also generously spent time discussing with me how she introduced Family Message Journals and why she uses them, and suggesting particular families' journals that might be interesting to investigate in depth, based on their diversity. These families, from both Dina's and Karen Wilensky's classrooms, trusted me with their journals and their perspectives on the strategy. As discussed in Chapter 6, they are excited about sharing their work and thoughts because they feel more teachers should be aware of the potential of Family Message Journals.

What I learned from Dina, Karen, the families, my classroom observations, and analysis of the journal messages helped me rethink and refine some of my own assumptions about writing instruction. As the process approach to writing instruction has begun to ossify into a set of rules, many teachers question their own judgment about how to promote writing development. This uncertainty persists despite experts' (such as Graves and Calkins) warnings not to treat suggestions as dogma or to interpret basic principles in a concrete fashion. I discovered there are important lessons to be learned about writing instruction from examining Family Message Journals and from exploring the thinking of two teachers who focus not on received wisdom about writing instruction but on thoughtful practice which encourages and supports children's full literacy development from the beginning of their school years. In this book I share my discoveries in the hope that they will spur other teachers to reflect on how they teach writing and how they might incorporate Family Message Journals into their programs, in *their own* ways.

Looking Ahead

Chapter 2 builds on issues of instructional philosophy raised in this chapter, taking a closer look at the theoretical foundation for Family Message Journals in what we know about literacy learning and instruction and about families' roles in their children's schooling. Chapter 3 presents a more practical focus on how Family Message Journals were implemented in Dina's and Karen's first-grade classrooms. Chapters 4 through 7 address what happened when the journals were implemented, both in the classrooms described and within the families highlighted in this book. The observations and sample messages discussed in these upcoming chapters shed further light on debates and issues surrounding writing instruction in general.

2 Why Family Message Journals? The Intersection of Writing Instruction, Writing to Learn, and Family Involvement

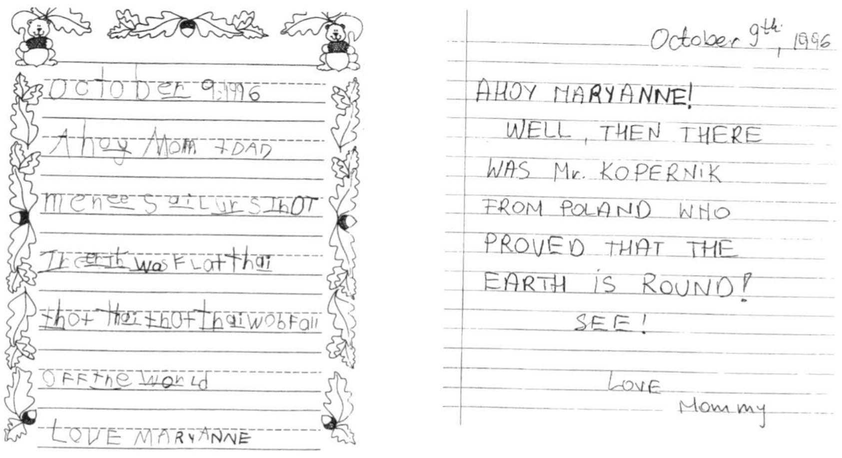

October 9, 1996
Ahoy Mom + Dad
Many sailors thought the earth was flat. They thought they would fall off the world.
Love Maryanne

October 9, 1996
Ahoy Maryanne!
    Well, then there was Mr. Kopernik from Poland who proved that the earth is round!
    See!
        Love,
            Mommy

Figure 2.1. This exchange between Maryanne and her mother demonstrates how sharing information with a real audience extends the learning process outside the classroom.

This chapter provides an overview of three strands of research and theory relevant to Family Message Journals. I look at what we know about writing development and instruction, the relationship between writing to learn and learning to write, and family involvement in student learning. In doing so, I build on issues touched upon in Chapter 1 and develop a theoretical foundation for using Family Message Journals. This foundation is important because it provides a base from which teachers can work to make the strategy their own, adapting it for their particular students and families while remaining faithful to their beliefs about literacy learning and to the research evidence. Further, this foundation provides a rationale, a response to those who might question whether Family Message Journals deserve a place in the curriculum.

What Do We Know about Writing Development and Instruction?

Teachers and researchers have long recognized that children learn to write by writing (Bissex, 1980; Calkins, 1994; Cambourne, 1988; Clay, 1975; Harste, Woodward, & Burke, 1984; Milz, 1985; Temple, Nathan, Burris, & Temple, 1988). Young writers need ongoing opportunities to experiment with print, trying to match sounds to letters and to express their ideas in writing legibly and clearly for themselves and for others. This is what Maryanne was doing when she deliberately worked out how to represent the long *e* sound at the end of *many* and the *r*-controlled vowel at the end of *sailor* so that her family would be able to read about what she had discovered that day at school (see Figure 2.1). If children need to write a lot to get better at it, then as teachers we need to give them many opportunities to write.

Not only do Family Message Journals provide daily opportunities for writing, but they also provide a real audience for that writing. Decades of research on writing development and instruction have shown that children need real purposes and audiences if their writing abilities are to develop fully and if they are to engage with writing as a worthwhile, motivating, lifelong activity (Calkins, 1994; Edelsky, Altwerger, & Flores, 1991; Routman, 1991). Writing for an audience *in* the classroom (peers) is often believed to provide a sense of purpose, but children also need to write for those outside the classroom and, for purposes of everyday life, to discover how writing works and what writing can accomplish in the world beyond school (Hall, 1998; Neumann & Roskos, 1991; Ryder, Vander Lei, & Roen, 1999). For

Maryanne the communicative value of her "flat earth" message lay in writing to a classroom outsider since her whole class had together discussed the surprising fact about sailors' fears—it was no longer "news" to her classmates and teacher. Although children may have a natural desire to communicate through writing (King & Rentel, 1979), teachers must create opportunities for them to do so and must help them see the many ways in which writing fulfills communicative needs (Ryder et al., 1999).

When a child is writing about school activities or learning in which the teacher or peers participated, teacher and peers may not constitute a real audience with whom to communicate—they already know what the writer knows. Families do not, however, and therefore constitute a more authentic audience, one in need of writing that is clear enough to communicate what happened if they weren't there. Family Message Journals are an opportunity for written dialogue that aids in the development of cognitive self-awareness and related appreciation of audience perspectives and needs.

Real purposes show children the value and uses of writing; real audiences provide communicative potential. The possibility that, through print, children can tell something they wish to tell or get something they want imbues writing with power. The potential of that power, however, lies in how successfully children communicate through their writing by anticipating audience perspectives and needs (Bereiter & Scardamalia, 1987; Frank, 1992; Harste et al., 1984; Kreeft, 1984; Langer, 1986; Ryder et al., 1999). While expressive writing, in which children state what is on their minds and what they are feeling, comes fairly naturally (Britton, 1970; Temple, et al., 1988), it is also natural for children to be unaware of whether their writing will communicate to others as intended. They have to learn that written language involves *anticipating* audience needs. They must elaborate sufficiently on their ideas to communicate clearly (Kreeft, 1984).

Sharing their writing with their families allows children to act on their desire to communicate with others (King & Rentel, 1979), while the responses provide feedback on the clarity and effect of their messages. Children can also learn a great deal about content, style, spelling, and other mechanics through writing to be understood and getting feedback on whether they were successful (Calkins, 1994; Harste et al., 1984; Milz, 1985; Ryder et al., 1999; Temple et al., 1988). So writing for a real audience encourages students to do their best—as Maryanne did when she painstakingly worked out spellings for the words she wished to use and considered what information to include in her message. The feedback she received from her mother reinforced the lesson that writing can be a powerful form of communication.

Unlike other home journals described in the professional literature (e.g., Shockley, Michalove, & Allen, 1995), Family Message Journals are truly examples of *children* writing to communicate. Children carry the full responsibility for the communicative value of their messages because teachers *do not* write in these journals at all. They are not for family-teacher communication (which, as discussed in Chapter 3, takes other forms in the classrooms I describe) but for family-child communication. In fact, many of the children's messages carried important information about school events and children's needs with respect to these events. One example is Kyle's message, accompanied by a series of stick-figure drawings showing a clothed figure losing his pants and eventually standing with bare legs:

> 11/6/96
> Mom and DAD MY Pears [pants] ar Foling DoWn and MY undWear to Ther Day NoVer [Thursday November] 9 is haT DaY I can Wear a HAT

After his playful opening, Kyle shared important information about an upcoming dress-up day at his school. He and his classmates did not want to forget to wear a hat on Thursday, especially since hats were usually not permitted in school.

The communicative value of the children's messages provides what first-grade teacher Dina Carolan describes as "built-in accountability" for doing one's best. Even if she can't read every child's journal every day, someone at home will, and this audience will provide immediate feedback about whether it is understood. When, for example, some of Kyle's early messages were difficult to read, his family told him it was hard to read messages when there were no spaces between the words. One of his mother's messages to him said, "I can't read what you wrote, try again." Kyle was able to read his message to his mother and get a written reply modeling conventions he was not yet using consistently, but at the same time his family also encouraged him to work at spacing and punctuation for easier communication through writing.

Writing Instruction—What Is a Teacher's Role?

Although we know that getting plenty of practice writing for real purposes and audiences is essential to writing development, it is not enough for teachers to simply let children write a lot; there is more to teaching than creating a facilitative, encouraging environment. Some learning may occur naturally, but introduction to and appropriation of new topics, forms, and purposes for writing often require careful guidance. Teachers play a crucial role in helping children move beyond what they *can* do and *choose* to do on their own (Applebee & Langer, 1983; Cazden, 1988; Langer & Applebee, 1986; Rogoff & Gardner, 1984; Vygotsky, 1978; Wood, Bruner, & Ross, 1976). Writing process advocates focus on teachers guiding children to revise writing on self-selected topics—frequently those representing or growing out of personal experiences—in self-selected genres, usually narrative (Calkins, 1994; Graves, 1983). But teachers can further challenge children and extend their writing abilities by assigning some topics for writing and by explicitly teaching them to write in a wide variety of genres.

Although established in Australia for more than a decade (Christie, 1985, 1986), the notion of teaching genres is only now gaining currency in the United States. Defining genre as "the different ways in which language patterns are realized in written texts to meet various social, communicative goals," Pappas and Pettegrew (1998, p. 36) argue that teachers must provide daily opportunities for students to write in various genres beyond the favored narrative. Daily and varied writing is important so that children learn the elements of "genres used in the different disciplines (science, math, and social studies)" that lend social validity to their writing (p. 42). Schleppegrell (1998), too, urges the explicit teaching of "linguistic features that make a particular text the type of text it is" (p. 183) rather than relying on the haphazard development of "intuitions" about how to structure different written forms which are "characteristic of different school subjects" (p. 185). We must teach children to write in ways that "make possible certain kinds of learning and social interaction" (Cooper, 1999, p. 25).

Teachers who provide a range of genre models and explicit instruction in genre characteristics, as well as practice in applying these, make new forms accessible to children. This accessibility not only gives child writers more choices of what and how they may write (Chapman, 1995), expanding their repertoires, but it also prepares them for upper-grade expectations that students will know how to write research papers, persuasive essays, scientific lab reports, poetry, and so forth. At the same time, as Hall (1998) argues, "privileging" certain forms of written language such as narrative divorces school literacy from real-life literacy:

> It is one of the paradoxes of schooling that the kinds of texts most privileged in schools are the ones least likely to be pursued once

people leave schooling. Most adults do not write stories, poems, or essays in their everyday lives. (p. 10)

Family Message Journals involve forms of writing typically privileged in secondary school, including essay and poetry writing, for which many elementary school children are ill-prepared, having written only narrative. But the journals also include many examples of the kinds of writing people do in their everyday lives outside of school, models we too often overlook in teaching writing. Chapters 4 and 5 explore in depth how children's messages are frequently used, for example, to list, instruct, request, persuade, or recall. Hall (1998) points out that these types of writing are often considered too difficult for young children; in any case, young writers are rarely if ever given opportunities to engage in creating such texts in school, despite the pervasiveness of these text types in the world outside of school.

If teachers do not intervene to provide direct instruction in writing, student experimentation with genre, topic, and function may be haphazard or nonexistent. Yet, as Dudley-Marling (1997) argues, balancing teachers' responsibility for such intervention with student ownership—intention and invention—is "complicated" (p. 75). It is important to note that the literature on teaching genre emphasizes that genre conventions are not rigid formulae but instead provide a range of choices—there is variation within any genre (Chapman, 1995; Schleppegrell, 1998). Similarly, teachers can honor students' intentions while expanding their knowledge and choices by assigning topics that are relevant to children's interests or concerns, or topics that contain flexibility and room for self-expression.

Teacher topic choice is a natural result of using writing across the curriculum. For example, every child might be asked to write about the results of a specific science experiment, as in Kristen's message which opens Chapter 1, or to report on information learned in a particular social studies activity, as in Maryanne's entry at the beginning of this chapter. In both cases, the student selected the information she would include and the way she would express it after various possibilities were shared during a class discussion that addressed both content and form for the particular type of message being composed.

When students use assigned topics and genres to write for genuine purposes and audiences, ownership need not be precluded. Rather, with Family Message Journals ownership grows out of the fact that the writing will be read by and will inform families and that immediate response is forthcoming. Children care about their writing because it communicates and compels response, not simply because they select what they are writing about and in what form.

What Do We Know about the Relationship between Writing to Learn and Learning to Write?

I noted previously that when teachers use writing as a tool for learning across the curriculum, they often ask students to write on assigned topics related to the content being explored. In this section I look at a second strand of research and theory that focuses on using writing as a tool for learning. The most common form such writing takes is the "learning log" or subject-area journal, often used in reading/literature study and social studies and used by some teachers in science and mathematics (Atwell, 1987, 1989; Avery, 1987; Fulwiler, 1982, 1987; Hancock, 1993; Wollman-Bonilla, 1989, 1991; Wollman-Bonilla & Werchadlo, 1995, 1999).

Writing in such logs or journals can help students stop and think about what they have learned and what questions remain. Writing, then, is a learner's tool for gathering and organizing thoughts. It nudges a student to articulate and shape ideas and sometimes helps a learner discover what she or he thinks. Additionally, because thoughts are put down on paper, letting the writer see and consider them, writing can help a student step back and reflect on information and ideas (Britton, 1970). Writing slows down our thought processes and helps us review and structure what we have learned (Emig, 1977). Maryanne's entry that opens this chapter is a simple example of how writing can help students reflect on a learning activity and put new knowledge into their own words.

At the same time, writing can promote learning by facilitating the process of expressing what we know and think so that we can connect our background knowledge and beliefs to new information. In Chapter 3 you will find many examples of children using writing to integrate new and abstract information with their own experiences. For example, in Family Message Journal entries the first graders connected learning about children in other places and times with their own daily experiences of grocery shopping, enjoying favorite foods, or engaging in play. Writing helped these students actively process information and make personal sense of it (Martin, D'Arcy, Newton, & Parker, 1976; Mayher & Lester, 1983).

Family Message Journals tap the power of writing as a tool for thinking, discovery, and self-expression—all important components of the learning process that undergird arguments for the value of journal writing in general. The kind of writing most often found in classroom journals is informal writing, which focuses on getting ideas down on paper and generating more ideas. Revision and editing are considered more appropriate for writing destined for formal presentation or classroom "publication." Britton and his colleagues (Britton, Burgess, Martin, McLeod, & Rosen, 1975) have described informal writing as "expressive" or "exploratory." Family Message Journal writing incorporates expressive personal writing with more formal explicit writing for an audience, reflecting attention to genre structure and linguistic conventions. In Britton's scheme, Family Message Journal entries fall somewhere on the continuum on which transactional (informative) and poetic (literary) writing represent opposite ends and expressive writing marks the middle (see Figure 2.2). That is, these journals constitute a format through which children work outward toward writing, as it is structured for various purposes and in various disciplines, by venturing away from the comfortable territory of expressive writing without losing its generative and reflective powers.

Kreeft (1984) describes the way in which informal dialogue journal writing helped a sixth-grade student move toward the audience demands of more formal, "essayist" prose, as opposed to oral conversation in which the listener is present. The teacher's feedback and encouragement to write about out-of-school activities in which she had not participated gradually helped the student adapt his writing to her needs as a reader. Family Message Journals help children recognize and enjoy the benefits of expressive writing while they create a bridge to formal writing (Kreeft, 1984). The intended audience's absence from the classroom forces the writer to strive for some degree of clarity, detail, organization, and convention. As children are writing to learn in Family Message Journals, they are simultaneously learning to write in fuller, clearer ways and in a range of forms.

What Do We Know about Family Involvement in Children's School Learning?

Clearly, families are key to the success of Family Message Journals—the existence of this audience and the feedback it provides transform the journals into tools for communication and growth in writing engagingly, explicitly, and conventionally. But there is more to family involvement in children's school learning than the convenience of families as correspondents. There is no shortage of research evidence

---

Functions of Writing[1]

Transactional < < < < Expressive > > > > Poetic

---

1. Adapted from Britton et al. (1975)

Figure 2.2. The functions of writing.

that involving families in flexible, convenient, and respectful ways boosts children's academic development and school performance (Cairney & Munsie, 1995; Epstein, 1991; Epstein & Dauber, 1991; Hoover-Dempsey & Sandler, 1997; Quint, 1994; Rosenholtz, 1989).

Yet, despite the value of family involvement, there are obstacles to overcome and myths to debunk before such involvement can be achieved. Obstacles include families' and teachers' attitudes and assumptions. Family members may be afraid to get involved because they did not do well in school themselves, did not attend school in this country and therefore find school expectations and norms unfamiliar and uncomfortable, or do not feel that their knowledge is valuable in a school context. A related problem is families' uncertainty about how best to help, even if they are willing and eager.

For their part, teachers must overcome a sense that relations with families are too often adversarial. Although a small minority of families may be antagonistic toward teachers and schools because of their life experiences and difficulties (Quint, 1994), the huge majority want the best for their children and will do whatever it takes to help them succeed in school. This includes low-income families, families of color, and families of minority cultural groups, all families too often assumed to have little or no interest in school (Baumann & Thomas, 1997; Delgado-Gaitan, 1990; Mulhern, 1997; Paratore, Melzi, & Krol-Sinclair, 1999; Quint, 1994; Taylor & Dorsey-Gaines, 1988). As Baumann and Thomas (1997) state, "cultural orientation, ethnic identity, or first language predicts little about family support for literacy and schooling" (p. 110). Despite the many assumptions muddying the waters of family involvement, research shows it is simply a myth "that parents do not take an active interest in their child's schooling" (Fact and Fiction, 1997/ 98, p. 7). So we must begin with the presumption that parents *do* want to get involved to help their children.

Informing Families

The short but necessary first step in family involvement is to inform families about school activities. They need to know what and how children are learning, and understand why, so that they can discuss and support classroom content and practices at home. Families should also be clearly and accurately informed about how children are doing—their strengths and areas needing improvement. Family Message Journals serve this dual goal: they tell families about school activities, and they provide a daily demonstration of each child's ability to produce clear, legible self-expression through writing, as well as a measure of each child's understanding of topics discussed in school. Maryanne's and Kyle's messages included earlier in this chapter indicate to their families where each one stands in writing development and in his or her grasp of the curriculum, or awareness of school events that have been discussed in their classrooms.

Inviting and Valuing Families' Participation

Moving beyond simply informing families, the second necessary step in family involvement is eliciting their participation in school curriculum and learning (Rosenholtz, 1989). Teachers need to build partnerships with families, involving them in school activities and also creating conditions in which students and the teacher can *learn from* the children's families. Rather than teachers always telling parents exactly what to do, the flow of information must go both ways (Cairney & Munsie, 1995; Delgado-Gaitan, 1990; Moll, 1992; Shockley et al., 1995). In order to take advantage of their ability to provide knowledge and support, we must assume that all families have something to contribute. An example is the reply to Maryanne's entry in Figure 2.1. Her family has new, related information to share about Mr. Kopernik (the Polish spelling for the astronomer Copernicus), an explorer who shares Maryanne's Polish heritage but who generally is not introduced in the first-grade curriculum. This message extended Maryanne's learning and that of her classmates when it was shared and discussed in school the next day.

While respect for what families have to offer is crucial, it is equally important to support their participation by clarifying for them how much their involvement is valued and the specific ways in which they can participate. Research tells us that families must receive a clear *invitation* to participate in their children's school learning; teachers must let families know they want to work with them as partners.

Otherwise, the adversarial assumptions and myths cannot be overcome (Epstein, 1986, 1991; Epstein & Dauber, 1991; Hoover-Dempsey & Sandler, 1997). Family Message Journals ask families to be crucial partners in school learning—families hold up one end of the correspondence *and* they teach through their messages.

We also know it is critical that families are clear about their roles; teachers' expectations for family participation should be made explicit. Families need to know exactly how they are being invited to help, why their participation is important, and how they can be effective in promoting children's school learning (Dauber & Epstein, 1993; Hoover-Dempsey & Sandler, 1997). Family Message Journals involve a clearly delineated mode of participation that is explicitly explained in letters from the teacher throughout the year. Samples of these letters are included in the next chapter. They explain that families' written replies to their children are an important indication that the children's messages command attention, but that they are also important to the children's growth in literacy and subject area knowledge. Further, these letters explain to families that they should write back *in response to* what the child wrote and that a short note is fine. This is meant to be a manageable task which can be completed in just a few minutes each day.

The final critical step in family involvement is to ensure that participation involves authentic learning from families (Rosenholtz, 1989; Shockley et al., 1995). Too often when we envision family involvement we think of families being instructed to drill children on arithmetic facts or sight-word flash cards. But family involvement should give families a true teaching or mentoring role rather than simply asking them to function as testers of knowledge assigned by the teacher. According to Dina Carolan, "The Message Journals involve both families and children in *learning*." This is evident in the reply to Maryanne's message about early sailors. Her mother assumed the role of teacher of new information related to what Maryanne learned in school that day. In this case the role allowed Maryanne's family to build on a classroom lesson by celebrating and confirming their heritage as valuable and relevant to what was happening in school.

It is also important to note that Maryanne's family played a key role in Maryanne's learning despite the fact that English is their second language; her mother and father are not fully comfortable writing in English—they are aware they make errors. But in Family Message Journals it is the family's knowledge and sharing of it that counts; participation in assisting children's learning is central. Teachers must recognize that families, too, can scaffold school learning, guiding children to know, understand, and do what they cannot yet accomplish on their own or have not yet been introduced to (Applebee & Langer, 1983; Cazden, 1988; Langer & Applebee, 1986; Rogoff & Gardner, 1984; Vygotsky, 1978; Wood, Bruner, & Ross, 1976). Chapter 6 provides many more examples of families teaching information and sharing insights related to the school curriculum.

Can It Work for *Any* Family?

Family Message Journals can make participation in children's school learning workable and comfortable for all families, regardless of makeup or background, because they participate from home at a time convenient for them. Writing a reply message takes only a few minutes, a small time commitment that most families can fit in at some point during the afternoon, evening, or early morning before school starts. Chapter 6 discusses what families told me about when and how they wrote, adding this activity to their already busy schedules.

Chapter 3 introduces the case-study families whose writing forms the foundation for this book. Chapters 4 and 5 provide many examples from the Family Message Journal entries of some of the diverse families in Dina Carolan's and Karen Wilensky's classrooms. They included families headed by a single parent, grandparent, or stepparent, as well as children with many siblings, no siblings, or siblings far removed in age. In some families the adults were still learning the English language, and languages other than English were spoken at home, as in Maryanne's. All of these families can participate comfortably in Family Message Journals. Of course, teachers need to be mindful and appreciative of potential difficulties, such as families' reluctance to expose their own weak writing skills or insecurity about writing in English when it is a second language. Teachers need to reassure families that it is the content of the reply that matters, not how conventional it is, and that replies are not evaluated but rather *appreciated* as a key component of the journal experience. Families may need some guidance in writing initial messages, and some may be invited to write in their home languages. More on this in the next chapter.

3 Family Message Journals in the Classroom

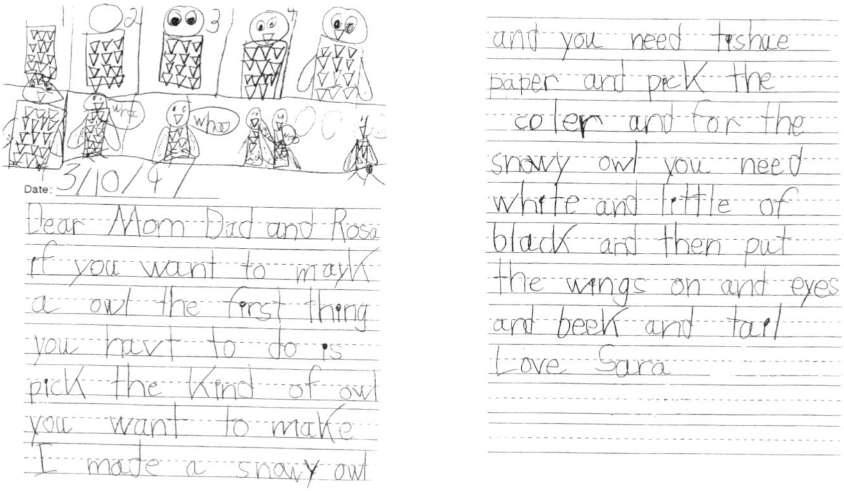

3/10/98
Dear Mom Dad and Rosa,
If you want to make a owl the first thing you have to do is pick the kind of owl you want to make. I made a snowy owl. And you need tissue paper, and pick the color. And for the snowy owl you need white, a little of black. And then put the wings on and eyes and beak and tail.
Love, Sara

Figure 3.1. Sara's "owl" message grew out of a unit of study that integrated multiple subject areas.

Sara's message in Figure 3.1 was written after she and her class-mates completed an arts and crafts activity related to a thematic unit on owls. In order to communicate clearly how she made the owl, she also drew a relatively elaborate diagram of each step in the process. This message is typical of the first graders' Family Message Journals in that it grew out of a unit of study integrating science, social studies, mathematics, literacy, and art. It also reflects the imperative to communicate clearly with readers—the child's family. How did the teachers guide their students to the point of being able to independently write relatively well-developed, extended, audience-friendly messages like this in the spring of first grade?

This chapter answers that question by focusing on the logistics of initiating Family Message Journals and exploring how they were used throughout the year as a context for teaching increasingly challenging writing techniques and conventions. My discussion of ways to implement the journals is grounded in observations of what Dina Carolan and Karen Wilensky did in their first-grade classrooms, and in discussions with these teachers. They have practiced and refined their approach until it works well, and they continue to refine it each year. Although I describe what these teachers did, I also explore other possibilities and consider how Family Message Journals might be adapted to other settings. In any case, all of the ideas here are suggestions—jumping-off points—to help others think about ways of implementing this strategy. Teachers who try to use Family Message Journals may find their own ways to do things that are better suited to their particular contexts, students, grade levels, and individual personalities and beliefs.

While Dina's and Karen's experiences can help others think about the potential of Family Message Journals, it is also important to explain exactly what they did so that readers can understand the context and procedures that gave rise to the children's and families' work highlighted in this book. I have argued that the basic approach these teachers used provided important instruction in and experience with writing. This chapter sets the scene, providing a backdrop against which to view the examples shared in upcoming chapters and to test my interpretations.

Gathering Information about Family Message Journals

I learned about Family Message Journals by acting as a participant-observer in Dina Carolan's classroom once a week from early October until late May. I watched as Dina asked children to write messages and as she discussed with them how and what they might write. And I watched and sometimes facilitated as the children wrote (e.g., guiding them to work out an invented spelling, providing encouragement by commenting with interest on what they had written, or asking a question to prompt elaboration). In this way, I was able to observe the children's processes and attitudes regarding the message writing, as well as to look on as many of them read, or reread, replies from home.

I also collected a number of artifacts from the classroom, including letters and notes sent home to parents regarding the Family Message Journals and other activities and expectations, the weekly class newsletter, and other materials used in conjunction with topics studied and written about in messages. For example, the health teacher distributed materials on oral hygiene, a topic that was extended into the classroom and formed the content of several Family Message Journal entries. Most important, I gathered the full, year-long corpus of Family Message Journal entries of four case-study students. This collection of the children's messages and their families' replies forms the foundation for this book. Finally, I informally interviewed the families and some of the first graders about Family Message Journals—how they used them, their attitudes about them, and their view of the journal's purpose.

With these multiple data sources, I was able to "test" my analysis of messages and replies, and my interpretations of what was happening, through triangulation among children's and families' written entries; my observations of classroom instruction and children's attitudes and behavior related to Family Message Journals; and teachers', families', and children's interview comments (Guba & Lincoln, 1981).

The School and Classroom Contexts

Dina Carolan and Karen Wilensky teach in a large elementary school situated in a sprawling, red-brick building in a suburb of Boston. The school enrolls about 630 children a year. The majority are Anglo, but the student body also includes about 7 percent African American students and about 3 percent Asian and 2 percent Latino/Latina students. Most students come from middle-class backgrounds, but working-class and upper-middle-class children are also well represented. The school has a policy of including special needs students in regular classrooms.

Dina's and Karen's classrooms are next door to each other and the two teachers work collaboratively, planning as a team, sharing their ideas, and "trading" their students for one afternoon each week to work with each other's groups. Karen has been teaching for many years; Dina was in her fourth year when I spent time in her classroom learning about Family Message Journals. Karen had introduced Dina to the idea of Family Message Journals, and the teachers regularly discussed procedures, problems, and successes and took turns composing related letters to families. Because I spent time in Dina's classroom, and because three of the four students whose work is highlighted here were her students, I will describe Dina's classroom. The teachers' classrooms were set up in similar fashion, however, so the description could easily fit Karen's classroom, in terms of both the physical environment and her philosophy and daily procedures.

The Physical Environment

The first thing I noticed on entering Dina's classroom was the amount of children's literature displayed around the room on windowsills, shelves, and the chalkboard tray and arranged in plastic baskets at each work table. Her extensive collection includes simple predictable books, picture books, and chapter books, as well as a range of literature-based basal readers from several different publishers.

In the classroom children sit in small groups at tables, and all supplies (pencils, crayons, markers, glue sticks, and paper) are shared by the classroom community. In the center of the tables sit old coffee cans full of sharpened pencils and plastic margarine tubs of crayons, along with baskets of books. The first graders in each of the table groups reflect mixed abilities and gender, and they rotate periodically so that children end up working in many different groups by year's end. Many small-group activities, such as science experiments and hands-on math explorations, take place at the tables. Most independent activities take place at the tables as well, including writing Family Message Journal entries. Children are encouraged to view their peers as well as their teacher as resources when questions or problems arise during independent or small-group activities. They are expected to help one another and converse quietly while working.

The first graders have a gathering area on the floor, complete with rug, for class meetings and small- and large-group lessons. They also often sprawl on the floor when pairing up to read to one another. All of the floor space is used in the classroom. Around the room Dina has set up a number of "discovery" areas—learning centers where students have an opportunity to explore and work with various arts and crafts as well as "academic" materials.

The room is enlivened with displays, charts, and posters of various sorts related to the current theme being studied and to mathematical representations of information, such as how many days the children have been in school. Frequently, displays include children's contributions—they are encouraged to bring in related objects from home. Print is everywhere—on walls, charts, and the chalkboard, including labels on objects, brainstormed lists of group-generated writing ideas, and facts learned about a topic of study.

A class pet, Brian the hamster, occupies one corner of the room, where children may take him out of his cage and play with him, learning how to treat a small animal gently and with respect. The room is on the first floor of the building, and a bank of windows extends along one entire wall, making it bright and sunny when the weather is nice.

The Students

The twenty-four students in Dina's 1996–97 first-grade class reflected the school's ethnic and socioeconomic makeup and included children receiving special services within and outside of the classroom, such as Title I, speech and physical therapy, and resource room support. Like any group of public school first graders, the children entered the classroom with a wide range of knowledge about literacy. Some were uncertain about the alphabet letters and about what to write when asked to do so; others were confident composers and inventive spellers who viewed themselves as people who could write and communicate through writing, even if they were aware that their writing was not always conventional.

The Family Message Journals of four case-study children— Kristen, Kyle, Maryanne, and Sara—are featured throughout this book. These children were selected by Dina Carolan and Karen Wilensky at year's end as individuals who, as a group, reflected the full range of writing ability in the first grade. My observations confirmed that these four students were representative, offering a microcosm of the classroom in terms of ability, sociocultural background, and general family attitude toward school involvement. Additionally, these children themselves graciously consented, as did their parents, to allow me to use their work in this book. The children included three girls and one boy who ranged in age from five to seven over the course of the first-grade school year. Two were emergent readers and writers (precommunicative spellers not yet able to consistently recognize and write conventional letter symbols); two were beginning readers and writers (using semiphonetic and phonetic spelling) as the school year opened.

All of the children lived in families in which both parents were employed, in occupations ranging from construction work and sales to academia and financial services. Thus they represented the socioeconomic diversity of their classroom. One child's family, Maryanne's, was bilingual, having come to the United States about ten years earlier. Their message journal communication was usually conducted in English, a language which Maryanne's parents were still working at learning. Each of the case-study children had at least one sibling. An older sibling served as correspondent in two of the Family Message Journals. Exploring the work of the case-study first graders provides a close look at Family Message Journals as a strategy for developing written communication skills, content-area learning, and family involvement in school.

The Teacher

Though one of the newer teachers in her school, Dina has already established a strong reputation. Among parents she is known as a warm, enthusiastic person and an excellent teacher with high standards. Children invariably label her "wicked nice"—the highest form of praise in the local dialect. In my experience, she is a teacher who demonstrates great energy, humor, patience, sensitivity, and dedication to her profession and her students. She is also generous in sharing her time and ideas with families. Both she and her colleague Karen have a strong commitment to family involvement in children's education. They make extensive use of parent volunteers on a daily basis so that all children are getting considerable small-group and one-on-one attention. They also assign homework that invites family participation and regularly inform families about curriculum and learning issues through handouts sent home as well as meetings in school. Additionally, they communicate with families through a weekly newsletter about what's been happening in the classroom and what to expect in the coming weeks.

The Curriculum

At the beginning of the year, Dina uses several handouts to inform families about her curriculum, approaches, and expectations. Dina's curriculum is theme centered, and she integrates all subject areas as much as possible, focusing throughout the day on oral and written language as important forms of communication and self-expression. Her reading program is literature based and involves independent reading, reading to partners, and listening to chapter books and picture books she reads aloud. She uses primarily trade books but also selectively employs fiction, nonfiction, and poetry from the literature-based basals available in her classroom. Children are given choice in what they read, but Dina provides guidance as needed to help her students select books which are manageable but challenging. Additionally, she employs a district-required phonics program for a period of about fifteen minutes each day. The program involves learning about the many sounds made by each letter and letter cluster, as well as dictation for assessment of students' auditory discrimination of different sounds and ability to match these to appropriate graphemes. Most students drew on this graphophonemic information at times to help them invent phonetic spellings while writing. This was evident when they chose a recently taught and plausible letter cluster to represent a sound in a word, sometimes over a simpler, correct letter or letter cluster (e.g., using *ough* for *oa,* which produced *roughd* for *road*).

The first graders are treated as readers and writers from the moment they enter the classroom. Dina works to ensure that they all find books they can read with some success from the start, and her wide collection of trade books allows her to meet individuals' needs. Students are also viewed as writers from day one, and they write a great deal in the classroom. In a handout, Dina reassures families that

> Initially much communication is done through pictorial representations and telling of stories. Then letters and words appear. Ultimately you will see sentences, and finally, written stories. Inventive spelling is allowed, accepted, and encouraged.

This handout is accompanied by a second one which explains the theory behind encouraging invented spelling and the stages of spelling development demonstrated by emergent to beginning writers.

Writing in the classroom revolves around Family Message Journals. At the beginning of the year, Family Message Journals are, in Dina's words, "about all they can handle," but by November children are also writing stories which are revised, edited, and published in the parent-run school publishing center. In the spring the first graders engage in a study of poetry, reading and writing in this genre. During the second half of the year, they also compose a word-processed weekly newsletter for families, with children working in pairs at the computer to write brief articles about particular classroom activities. (During the first half of the year, the teachers write the newsletter.) Children also regularly use the computer to compose stories. Some of their Family Message Journal entries are word processed, though most are handwritten; the school has a limited number of computers. Access is slowly improving, however, and increasingly children are composing on the computer. Even with their various other writing activities, by the end of the year the majority of children's school writing continues to consist of increasingly lengthy daily Family Message Journal messages.

Although Dina accepts every child's attempt at writing, no matter how unconventional in the beginning, her attitude that they *can* write, and the many demonstrations and opportunities for practice she provides, result in nearly all of them writing words—and some writing sentences in invented spelling—within the first weeks of school. Penmanship is given attention within the context of all writing for real audiences, as well as through formal instruction, as needed.

Mathematics and science are taught primarily through hands-on activities, problem solving, demonstrations, and manipulatives, including real-world objects such as coins. As Dina explains to families in her September handout, the first graders work on real-world problems such as figuring out the weight of objects to be used in a science experiment, creating story problems relevant to children's lives and questions, and working with the calendar. These experiences and others help them develop concepts of "patterning, sequencing, numeration, odd and even, place value, grouping, coin currency, graphing, and the formation of equations." Math and science are integrated and often revolve around classroom themes. Writing is used extensively in both areas. For example, many science experiments involve the use of a "Prediction" sheet, with large spaces to fill in "Here's what I think will happen" beforehand and "Here's what happened" after completing the experiment. Sometimes these prediction sheets are then used to compose entries for the Family Message Journals.

Social studies is taught primarily through trade books as well as "The Weekly Reader" children's newspaper and other hands-on and print resources used as "stimuli for discussions," in Dina's words. Like math and science, social studies is theme centered. Theme-related materials that children bring from home are always welcomed and given full attention. Art and crafts projects are often part of classroom units or literature-response activities. Themes are sometimes coordinated with "special" teachers, particularly the health teacher, but also with the art and music educators at times.

Family Message Journals are integrated into all curriculum areas in Dina's and Karen's classrooms and constitute a major focus of the literacy curriculum, as noted earlier. Journal entries are based on a range of learning experiences, including reading from trade and text books, brochures, and "The Weekly Reader"; group discussion; special presentations; hands-on observation or experimentation; problem solving; and individual thinking and imagining. Assigned topics and genres require children to write on a regular basis about activities and knowledge related to all subject areas. The teachers deliberately plan for the children to write on a wide range of subjects because writing helps them learn in all areas while also exploring the various types of writing used in specific disciplines and for specific real-world purposes.

The Content of Family Message Journals

Family Message Journal entries encompass a wide variety of topics. Though many entries, such as Sara's "owl" message in Figure 3.1, are related to integrated units of study, others are simply responses to independent reading selections or read-alouds; responses to prompts

Table 3.1. Topics of First Graders' Messages over the Course of One School Year

Topic[1]		Number of Messages
Science		41
Weather, Seasons	13	
Animal Behavior & Habitats	12	
Experiments, Structured Observations	9	
Reading & Discussion of Other Topics	7	
Special Events—Assemblies, Trips, Dress-Up Days		25
Response to Literature		16
Social Studies		15
History & Cultural Traditions	11	
Current Events	4	
Personal Feelings & Memories, Managing Emotions		12
Health, Hygiene, Safety		10
Language Arts—Story Writing, Spelling, Letter Formation		10
Mathematics		8
Personal Wishes & Goals		4
Total		141

1. Genres and functions of messages varied within each topic category, as discussed in Chapters 3, 4, and 5.

related to social studies discussions focusing on self-awareness, self-esteem, and cooperation; descriptions of special school events; or postvacation thank you notes expressing appreciation for vacation activities. The teachers plan topic assignments as they plan weekly and monthly curriculum:

> We usually know what the children will be writing about at least a week ahead. Of course that can change. Like when an assembly is announced at the last minute, and it's on a good topic for a message. Or if something comes up in discussion. We have to be flexible.

Table 3.1 lists the general topics of entries written in one year in Dina Carolan's first-grade classroom. Although the table offers a picture of the many different things children were assigned to write about, this is a simplified overview that does not do justice to the content of each entry in the way the actual examples do. Many entries were related to multiple subject areas and had more than one topic and function, defying traditional categorization. For example, Sara's owl message was related to a unit on owls that involved reading and writing nonfiction and fiction; learning about owls' behavior, senses, anatomy, and adaptation to different environments; observing and dissecting owl pellets; learning about owl habitats and human infringement on them; categorizing and graphing owls according to their appearance, popularity, and frequency; and engaging in arts and crafts activities like the one Sara described. Of course, the curriculum is always evolving and changing somewhat to meet students' needs, address their interests, and reflect current events, so the list in Table 3.1 would not be exactly the same another year.

What remains the same from year to year is Dina's and Karen's commitment to organizing learning thematically in their first-grade classrooms. Thus it is typical for messages to be related to multiple curriculum areas. A fully fleshed-out example might help illuminate how this happens. In a thematic unit on the current season, autumn (part of a year-long curricular focus on the changing seasons), children might sort, count, and graph how many leaves of each color they collected on an autumn nature walk. This collection and graph would be linked to explorations of why and how leaves change color and how people's behavior also changes with the seasons. Finally, children might learn about places where the coming of autumn results in very little change in climate, behavior, or environmental scenery or in changes quite different from those which are familiar to New Englanders.

Such a unit would spawn various Family Message Journal entries over the course of several weeks. For example, children might write about the following:

1. scientific observations from their nature walk to collect leaves

2. the results of their graphing and how graphs represent mathematical information

3. their hypotheses about the reason for their findings on leaf color distribution

4. subsequent reading they do about why and how leaves change color

5. whether their knowledge of why and how leaves change suggests a reason for leaf color distribution, comparing their original hypotheses with their new information

6. their personal feelings about autumn and favorite seasonal activities

7. how autumn weather affects people's behavior where they live

8. reading they do about autumn in other places, in comparison with how the season manifests itself where they live

9. images of autumn in the form of a poem

10. a visit from a scientist-parent who studies animal behavior and discusses how various animals adapt to the arrival of cold weather

11. their own autumn adventure in a fictional story

This series of messages incorporates—and individual messages often integrate—mathematics, science, and social studies concepts, reading, and, of course, writing. This degree of integration could be achieved using Family Message Journals at any grade level, around any grade-appropriate theme.

The journal itself connects related learning experiences. With messages physically layered and thematically interwoven, the journal can help children recognize connections across a variety of traditional disciplines; through the consistent medium of the daily journal message, they can focus on different facets of a topic or means of finding out about it. As a collection of entries, the journal can serve as a record of learning around specific themes that are the topic of multiple messages.

Writing is not only the medium of the journals but also the focus of instruction. In the process of writing the eleven messages listed previously, for example, children would be guided in exploring the relatively new genres of poetry, exposition, and scientific writing. Some messages might consist of simple lists of facts; others might be formatted in two parts: "Here's what I think" and "Here's what I found out." Still others might be written in the form of a song or story. Most often the type of writing is part of the assignment, and the first-grade teachers talk with their students about how to structure their messages.

The reading of several poems about seasons, for example, and discussion of what makes a poem a poem preceded the students' writing of their own "That Was Fall" poems, modeled after the final verse of Marci Ridlon's (1969) "That Was Summer." This verse begins: "Have you ever smelled summer?" and ends: "Remember how warm the soil smelled/and the grass?/That was summer." The first graders' poems all followed Ridlon's form to some extent and contained sensual images, but each one highlighted what the writer felt was special about or unique to fall. Sara wrote:

That Was Fall

Have You ever Smelled fall
Lik aPPle Pie
and fresh cool air
That was fall

The first graders' journal entries during the time they were introduced to and required to try out various genres exhibit many examples of independent genre exploration. When given the freedom to choose, some chose to write messages expressing their ideas in the form of a poem or song rather than a narrative. For example, in one year-end message students were asked to think back on their first-grade experience and examine their feelings about school ending for the summer. Kristen decided to write a poem, which appears to be influenced by a poem the class had read earlier in the week, "Good Books, Good Times!" by Lee Bennett Hopkins (1990):

> Dear family,
> I'm going to call this poim my first grade Book
> I'm sad I have to leave school
> I met a lot of friends
> I herd a lot of stories
> Good times and good people
> Love Kristen

Other children wrote messages that took the form of riddles or jokes, or incorporated these forms into narrative messages. Kyle frequently included jokes in his Family Message Journal. In one message he recounted some of what he had learned during a class study of spiders:

> Dear mom Did you know that a spietr is a vapier [vampire] caus
> it suks the Boold [blood] from inceks two are poson [poison] some
> are red purple spider do not have wing spiter have two body
> parts Male spider are smaller than femals love Kyle

Kyle enlivened his list of facts with a joke about spiders being like blood-sucking vampires. Many children in the first-grade classrooms experimented naturally with genre when given the opportunity to do so.

I suspect, however, that their experimentation was a result of their exposure to a wide range of genres and the requirement that they try them all out. Their teachers deliberately introduced them to many types of writing and invited them to see how they worked. Many messages called for specific genres, such as a story or an expository report on findings of an exploration. Even then there was room for experimentation with form, as Maryanne's journal shows. Communicating facts learned from a November study of Native Americans, she wrote:

> November 22, 1996
> Dear Mom + Dad,
> 1. N.A. [Native Americans] played snow snak.

2. N.A. hade no shaws [a local grocery store chain].
3. N.A. hade boas and aroas.
Love, Maryanne

A message written less than a month later comparing the two winter holidays celebrated by children in Maryanne's class read:

December 19, 1996
Dear Parents,
Hi. The class founed out that Crictmas and Hounica are very much alike. Thay bothe inclood prezents and ornameints. Love Maryanne

Both messages involve taking stock of the information she has learned and relating it to her own knowledge and experiences, but she tries out different formats—an enumerated list and a narrative—which had been modeled and discussed in her classroom.

Because they cut across the curriculum and disciplinary areas that are characterized by distinct types of writing, Family Message Journals are a context for learning about different ways to express ideas and information, as well as for rethinking and recording what was learned. Like Dina and Karen, teachers can introduce, demonstrate, and discuss specific genres, or ways of representing information and ideas in writing, especially within the framework of subject areas which involve specialized forms of writing.

Initiating Family Message Journals

In a recent article, Bomer (1998) describes approaches to explicit instruction that give teaching true "learning value." He argues that effective literacy teaching entails "demonstration" of the process of writing. Teachers must enact, in front of their students, the decision making that writers struggle with. Further, teachers must provide conditions for "assisted performance." As Bomer explains, rather than *tell* students how to perform a writing task, ask them to *do* it and support them as they try. Finally, Bomer writes, teachers must make room for "reflective description," in which students are asked to talk about what they have done while working independently. Articulating what one has done builds conscious awareness of how to apply processes and techniques demonstrated by the teacher or shared by a peer. Such articulation gives the writer greater control and demonstrates for peers how they might attempt the same process or technique. This reflection on work attempted often takes place during a whole class sharing time but may also occur during a one-on-one conference with the teacher. Bomer's framework of demonstration, assisted performance, and reflective description, is useful in discussing how the first-grade teachers initiated Family Message Journals.

Introducing the Journals: Demonstration

During the first weeks of school in September 1996, Dina introduced Family Message Journals to her students by saying, "You will be writing a letter to your family about things you do in school." She then explicitly demonstrated how to write a Family Message Journal entry before she asked her students to attempt one. She assigned herself a topic from that day's activities in school and asked herself aloud, "What are all the things I could write about it?" With the children's input—they brainstormed ideas and discussed the value of each suggestion offered—she decided on what might be most important to tell someone who was not in the classroom for the activity.

Some preliminary content decisions made, she then wondered aloud how to format her message. Writing in front of her students at an easel, she talked about using a letter format and created a sample, which was left hanging up for children to refer to. She suggested some possible greetings, such as "Hi Family," "Dear Mom," "Dear Dad," or "Dear Grandma," and then invited the children to suggest others. She encouraged greetings which might grab readers' attention. For example, a message about a health lesson focusing on the heart and how many times it beats each minute might begin, "Boom, boom Mom and Dad."

Dina proceeded to write her message, thinking aloud about her final content decisions as well as modeling how to listen for the sounds in a word and write an invented spelling. Finally, she discussed how she might close her message.

Students Begin Their Own Messages: Assisted Performance

After the demonstration, students were invited to begin writing their own messages on a topic discussed earlier in the day—the colors in a rainbow. As the children wrote, Dina circulated, assisting their performance. She encouraged them to spell as best they could rather than expect her to tell them how to spell every word, and she also reminded them that many words they might want to use were included in the sample entry she had written or on the word wall in the classroom. She urged students to use these resources. When the first students announced they were finished, she asked them if there was anything they might add to make the message clearer to family members or to provide helpful detail. Some did add a bit; others chose not to.

At the beginning of the year during which I observed Dina's classroom, the first graders wrote messages only twice a week; now, however, Dina and Karen begin daily writing from the start of the school year to provide increased practice with writing and to instill the habit of writing to communicate, as well as to establish families' replying routine. At first it took about forty-five minutes to an hour for Dina to provide the instructional support students needed to get started each day and to give them plenty of time to compose their own messages. Most of the messages written during the first month were just one sentence long, like Kristen's response to *Chicka Chicka Boom Boom* (Martin & Archambault, 1989):

> 9/16/96 Chicka Chicka Boom Boom
> I.liked.black.I.pee.

Nevertheless, from the beginning the first graders were encouraged to use as many sheets of paper as necessary for a single message, and it did not take long—a month or two—before some students were writing multiple-sentence and multiple-page entries. Others continued for months to write messages consisting of only one or two sentences. Each student was encouraged to write as much as possible and to reread and add to the original message she or he had created before taking it home, but individual needs were always taken into account in Dina's expectations for message length and general attentiveness to writing.

When they finished writing, children illustrated their messages, and when that was completed each student inserted the loose-leaf message into a slim three-ring binder. In order to avoid loss of a Family Message Journal, Dina carefully instructed children to make sure their binders "live in your backpack, come out for a visit at home, and go to bed in your backpack." These instructions have worked; a Family Message Journal has never been lost!

At the beginning of the year, most of the children drew a picture to go with every message—they were still grounded in the notion that drawings communicate equally, or at least in a fairly even balance, with print. By the end of the year, pictures were rare, unless they were diagrams that were a component of the message, as in Sara's entry in Figure 3.1. In part, this is a result of the paper students were offered. Early in the year, they were given paper with space for pictures at the top. Later, the paper they used was fully lined, though they could, and very occasionally did, draw on this.

Initially, a few children resisted writing because they felt they could not do it. One-on-one or small-group assistance from the teacher or a classroom volunteer usually helped these children get started. They had ideas to write about but needed help listening for the sounds in the words they wanted to use and deciding on the letters to represent those sounds. Having already seen their teacher demonstrate the process of making such decisions, students quickly became comfortable with not being sure of spellings and doing their best to write down ideas. Any resistance to writing rapidly vanished as students took home their first few messages and received replies. The feedback was encouraging for all, as was the new-found self-esteem of becoming one who can truly communicate through writing with grown-ups and older siblings. Dina found that within a few weeks the entire class *asked* for time to write in their Family Message Journals and protested if they did not have time to do so each day.

As in many primary classrooms, a handful of first graders did not yet write conventional letter symbols, and even more students were precommunicative (prephonetic) spellers. For one or two children, fine motor development interfered with the clarity of their handwriting, making it difficult for family members to decipher a message. Rather than taking dictation from these children, Dina encouraged them to write as best they could, giving them much-needed practice in writing and thinking about letter-sound correspondences. Then, if necessary—and this depended on the child and how well he or she could remember the message's content—Dina might write a "translation" on a sticky note affixed to the entry to help families formulate a reply. Most children, however, were able to remember what they wrote *about*, if not what they intended word for word (and here drawings helped), so they were able to initiate discussion with family members about an entry without a teacher's translation. Dina and Karen prefer not to provide translations because they want the children to feel that their writing stands on its own from the start, but for a small number of children at the very beginning of the year translations may be helpful in communicating with families and compelling response.

Special needs students who cannot print on their own because of motor disabilities are sometimes successful when composing messages on a computer, assisted by an aide, teacher, or peer who has been coached on how to help without controlling. If word processing messages is not feasible, teachers may need to take dictation from these students so that they too can participate in the exchange of messages.

Sharing Messages and Families' Replies: Reflective Description

Sometimes immediately after writing and sometimes as part of the next day's minilesson before writing, students engaged in "reflective description"—talking about what information they had included in their messages and why, sharing various sorts of greetings, or talking about how they "got" the spelling of a tricky word. Students were also invited to read aloud their complete messages, and they learned from each other about new possibilities for content and form.

During the third week of school, in a typical reflective discussion, students shared their many ideas for grabbing readers' attention with a message greeting and came up with a brainstormed list, which was then posted in the classroom for future reference. The list, which I copied from the wall in late September, included all-purpose greetings and greetings for messages about animals ("Grrr" and "Squeak"), the weather ("Brrr"), Hat Day at school ("Hats off to you"), and science experiments ("Surprise" and "Abracadabra"):

Yo	Greetings
Dear family	Hey
What's Up	Dear
Hi	Yoo Hoo
Hello	Grrr
Abracadabra	Surprise
Hats off to you	Hocus pocus
Hi ho	Wow!
Squeak	Brrr

Demonstrations by the teacher and reflective descriptions by students provided additions to this list throughout the year. The first graders added greetings in other languages, such as "Bonjour" and "Hola," some of which were introduced by family members in their reply messages. Once introduced, students began to pick up on one another's models and try greetings in their home languages or a familiar second language.

Each day students were given time to read their families' latest messages before they began writing a new one, and the teacher often encouraged them to read aloud what their families had written, either within their small groups or to the whole class. Family reply messages not only initiated valuable reflective discussions, but they also prompted some explicit instruction. For example, Dina noted that Kyle's father had used his message to tell a joke, or Kristen's mother used her message to explain how to do something, giving specific directions, so that Kristen and her classmates would be able to do it after reading the message. She made the families' messages part of the curriculum, teaching new techniques by highlighting their use in families' replies.

The Journals as a Context for Continuing Instruction in Writing

After about a month, students began to write messages more often and soon were writing daily. Even those who began writing indecipherable messages with invented letter symbols or precommunicative spelling began to use semiphonetic spellings which were decipherable to their teacher. Once the Family Message Journals were established, Dina's process of demonstration, assisted performance, and reflective description remained constant, but her demonstrations focused on new areas, and the time required both for explicit instruction and for writing decreased, in part because of the children's growing confidence and ability in writing. Dina's models created during demonstration were not always as complete as in the first weeks, but students no longer needed this degree of support. Also, she found that complete models began to interfere with students writing their own messages because some treated the models as an example to copy word for word. By year's end the entire process of instruction, writing, and sharing by a few children took only about twenty to twenty-five minutes.

As children became comfortable with their journals, the teachers began to tap the journals' full power as an instructional context. New areas which Dina began to specifically introduce after a month or two included audience awareness (encompassing the need for explanation and elaboration) and the use of capitalization and simple punctuation to make messages clearer for readers.

From the start of journal writing, the first graders read over their messages before they took them home. While the children wrote, their teachers circulated through the room to read as many as they could, asking questions and encouraging elaboration in an effort to develop audience awareness. But the teachers' expectations grew and changed over time, as their minilessons and feedback to students indicated. They began to raise and discuss in detail expectations for content, asking questions such as, "What does your family have to know about the experiment?" and "Is it okay if you forget to tell them it involved apples? Will your message still be clear?"

Demonstrations also helped students develop clearer, more complete messages. For example, Dina wrote a few messages that were missing crucial information and asked the students for help with improving them. Eventually, she told students that every message must include "three specific pieces of information" and explained and demonstrated what she meant, suggesting that "it is cool" and similar general statements are not very informative. Sara's message describing a science activity in which her class engaged—dissecting an owl pellet as part of a unit on owls—reflects her teacher's encouragement to include at least three pieces of specific information.

> 2/26/97
> Hoo hoo Mom Dad and Rosa
> owl pelits kum from owls. and they kawf it uP the day after
> they eat it. and the things they kawf uP are teeth, fer, boans,
> and tails. and it can kawf uP Parts av fish, snakes and skunks.
> Love sara Dear Mom Dad and Rosa I saw wut was insighd a
> owl Pelit. I want to go to the wuds to finde one. Love sara

Sara not only worked to include at least three specific pieces of information, but she also realized when she reread her entry that she had forgotten some important information—she had actually dissected an owl pellet with her small group! She added this to her entry (with a brand new greeting!), again reflecting her teacher's repeated emphasis on and demonstration of how to include all of the important information in a message. Dina's observations of what the children did in their writing prompted new minilessons. For example, Sara's approach to adding more information led Dina to explain conventions for adding additional information at the end of a letter, using "P.S." instead of a new greeting.

Dina also wrote messages with no capital letters or punctuation and read them aloud, discussing why she felt she needed to go back and work on these mechanics—to aid communication—and then doing it in front of her students. Some lessons focused on using various resources and strategies for spelling (including the invitation to collaborate with peers to figure out spellings) and on the value of neat handwriting to facilitate communication. These lessons sometimes drew on related classroom lessons on punctuation, spelling, and handwriting. Family Message Journals provided a context in which children could see why these conventions matter and apply what they had learned to purposeful communication.

Other minilesson demonstrations and discussions focused on using new vocabulary appropriate to the content area or genre of the message. For example, in March when the first graders studied wind they were introduced to some new words from the vocabulary of meteorology. They talked about words to use in place of *windy* that would be more specific and accurate to describe the nature of the wind, and whether the wind is benign or dangerous and destructive. Whenever new content-area vocabulary was introduced, students were encouraged to think about using some of the new words in their messages. A brainstormed list of wind-related words, complemented by a list of meteorological terms for types of wind events, provided a resource for students to refer to when writing. Family Message Journals gave them an opportunity to try out new words in a context that encouraged this experimentation, and students were eager because they wanted to impress their families with their sophisticated vocabularies.

> 3/3/97
> Dear Mom Dad and Rosa
> March is a windy munth of the year and if you had your hands
> out it feels like the wind is pushing you and it is veiry blustery
> Love Sara

Sara tried out the word *blustery* and received positive feedback from her father in his reply message:

> 3/3/97
> Dear Sara,
> I like the word "blustery." People who talk loudly are some-
> times called blustery, too. Do you know any blustery people?
> Love, Papa

This is a good example of how families contributed to the curriculum—teaching through their messages—a topic expanded on in Chapter 6.

Dina also used prewriting minilessons to discuss and demonstrate conventions of different genres. Students watched and listened to her think aloud as she formatted and organized a brief report on a science experiment involving apples and then a poem on apples. She discussed organizing messages around hypothesis-finding statements ("I think" and "I found out"), in list or narrative form, and as a story of an event or a "just-the-facts" report; and she addressed related stylistic issues. For example, what is the best way to begin a message in which you ask for something from a family member? Should you simply ask, demand, persuade, or state *why* you need it? Which is likely to be most effective?

More challenging minilessons were accompanied by assisted performance in which Dina also raised her expectations as the year progressed and individual students showed signs of readiness for greater challenge. Whereas initially she provided a great deal of positive feedback, over time as she circulated among the journal writers she began to say to certain students, "You can write more," or "Let's see if you can write to the bottom of the page," or "Go on to the back of the paper." These challenges pushed some students to go beyond what had become their routine of writing only two sentences per message, for example, and addressed the fact that some children interpret directions to "write at least three pieces of information" as indicating not only what is necessary but also what is sufficient, and so they limit themselves.

Reflective description continued as well, as students were told that each day some of them would be chosen to share their messages and talk about what they did that was new or that illustrated the day's minilesson. Sharing with a preliminary audience (before families saw the messages) provided further motivation to do one's best and gain classmates' attention and interest. Dina also noted that students learned a great deal from each other about new writing techniques, style, and development of ideas, and also about the subject-area content of the entry. Each child's memories of and comments on any particular activity varied somewhat, and only some of these had been shared during prewriting brainstorming discussions. After giving students an opportunity to share during reflective description, Dina tried to call attention to what children had done in their writing and to what they had recalled, in order to make their listening peers aware. This awareness gave all students a wider range of tools and techniques they could consciously select from when writing.

Family Message Journals provide a purpose and a meaningful context for instruction in writing, challenging children to grow as writers and expanding their knowledge of how to write well and effectively. But what happens in the classroom is only one piece of the picture.

Introducing the Journals to Families

Because Family Message Journals may be unlike anything families have been asked to do by their children's school, and because family participation is so important, the journals must be carefully and clearly introduced to families. Family members need to know what is expected of them and why.

First, families need to understand and appreciate children's invented spelling. Otherwise, the children's messages simply look wrong to family members, and concern and criticism grow with each message. Even though Dina and Karen provided considerable information for families about invented spelling at the beginning of the school year, many family members still questioned their children's writing, worrying that messages were reflective of a language disability and sometimes communicating their worries to their children, if only subtly. Dina and Karen find they must meet in individual conferences with at least several parents, grandparents, or guardians each year to reassure them that the writing in their children's messages is normal. They make it clear they are open to such meetings, whether the conferences are formally scheduled or informal, as family members simply stop by before or after school.

Second, Dina and Karen reassured families that they might not be able to read children's messages early in the year and that this is okay. Nevertheless, they explained (in a general letter to families about classroom expectations and procedures), it is extremely important to write back to show children that writing is a valued and effective form of communication. They recommended that families ask a child to "read me your message," explaining that even if what the child "reads" is not what he or she intended to write, the child is still engaging in communication. And if a child cannot "read" or remember what was written, that is okay, too. Though the goal is that family replies be relevant to the child's message, it is *crucial* that families show interest in the child's efforts and that they reply—that they write *something*. In part this provides what Dina calls "some accountability"; children care about their messages because they know someone at home is going to pay attention to them. More important, it reinforces the idea that writing communicates, even for emergent writers. And, of course, families' writing usually provides a daily model of conventions for each child, complementing the text models they are exploring in school.

In order to make sure that families understood what they were being asked to do and why, after the teachers' initial introduction of Family Message Journals and their importance in children's learning, a letter was sent home with the child's first journal entry. The letter was typed by the teacher, signed by the child, and inserted in the binder, the physical embodiment of the journal, followed by the child's first message. The letter read:

> Dear Family,
>   This is my message journal notebook. I will be bringing it home everyday. Ask me to tell you about my drawing and message. Please print a short note back to me. Go over your note with me a few times to reinforce my reading skills. I will reread your message to the teacher each day. It is requested that the family member PRINT the message, "modeling" a letter format. Include the

date, a greeting, the body, a closing and a signature, please. I need
to bring my journal safely back to school the very next day.
                              Sincerely,

This letter was an important reminder of what the teachers had already
explained in a previous newsletter about families' writing aiding children with their literacy learning.

The letter also provided an explanation of what was expected of
families. Because families wonder whether anyone else will see what
they write, the teachers were clear from the start that they would read
the messages with the children. Some families did not know that a letter
format was appropriate and were surprised and thankful for this bit of
guidance, saying, "I never would have realized I should write my
message that way." For families unfamiliar with a letter format, one
model was provided by the child's initial messages. Teachers may also
send home an additional format guide if they find, after reading several
family replies, that this support would be helpful.

Dina and Karen did not begin the year by suggesting certain
types of messages, because they wanted families to share what they felt
was important and not feel constrained by a list of ideas. If a family
member asked what he or she should write, the teachers discussed
possibilities but made it clear there was no single correct approach.
Occasionally, families attached notes to their messages asking if they
were "okay," and the teachers reassured them with a note back,
sometimes taking the opportunity to make further suggestions for
replies, such as sharing related information from the family heritage or
about special skills, or remembering to provide positive feedback to a
child, as well as sharing knowledge.

Since the year I spent in their classrooms, Dina and Karen have
found it helpful to send home a model message and reply to show
families what it means to "reply to the child's message topic." As Dina
recently explained to me:

> If the child's message is about arctic animals and a parent writes
> back about having pizza for dinner, then they aren't getting the
> point. They aren't really *communicating* with their child through
> writing, and they aren't taking the child's writing *seriously* by re-
> acting to what the message is actually about.

That parent is also missing the opportunity to use the reply to contribute
to the child's school learning.

As noted earlier in this chapter, families made up of English language learners may need reassurance that their best efforts to write in

English are fine and that writing in the home language is fine, too. These are issues the teachers address as they arise, but in schools where there are many bilingual families or families that prefer a language other than English, teachers might want to begin the year by inviting them to write in whatever language they choose, discussing the value of sharing and maintaining the home language.

Several times Karen has worked with children whose families are not literate in any language, and this may be a common situation for some teachers. Inviting such families to draw replies or give them orally might be good approaches in this case. If the first grader can do so, he or she might even take dictation from a family member. Of course, many families in which parents, grandparents, or other adults may not be literate include literate older siblings who can also contribute by writing messages or taking dictation from parents. Karen also found that when her first graders wrote to their illiterate parents, the parents began to take an active interest in learning to read, and the first graders actually used their messages to begin to teach their parents to read!

In a class of about twenty-four students, Dina and Karen have found that about twenty families write messages back every single day, and nearly all write back on a regular basis (at least twice a week). However, there is often one family per class that never writes back, and this number might be higher in a different school context. To provide the experience of written communication to students who do not receive family replies, and to reinforce their efforts at writing, the teachers select or ask the child to select another correspondent. In order to "make families accountable, and help them understand how important daily replies are, because the kids need to see that their writing is important," Dina and Karen now send home an additional note at the beginning of the school year informing families that if they can't meet the expectation for regular replies, the teachers "will find someone who *will* write back." These other correspondents have included the school's Title I or resource teachers, "special subject" (art, gym, health, or music) teachers, student teachers, teacher-education students, school volunteers, and older students (fourth or fifth graders).

As the introductory letter sent home indicates, families are encouraged to read and discuss their replies with the first graders at home, though children are also given time to reread and share the messages in school the next day. Chapter 6 addresses families' strategies for finding time to write and share the messages despite their busy schedules.

Dina and Karen have also found that sending home periodic letters reminding families of the expectation that they reply and that the journal make it back to school each day helps keep participation high. After about two months, the following letter was sent home, as children "graduated" to Family Message Journal binders with greater capacity:

> Dear Family,
>   This is my new Message Journal. I will be responsible for bringing this journal and my reading homework to school each morning. Space should be available for you to write an answer on the *back* of my message.
>   Thank you!

Like the first one, this letter was typed by the teachers and signed by the children. It not only served as a reminder, but it also indicated that students were starting to write longer messages, and replies would need to go on the back of the child's message or, as some families began to do, on a separate piece of paper inserted in the binder.

In January, after the holiday vacation, yet another reminder and information letter was sent home:

> Dear Family,
>   Happy New Year! We will be cleaning out our message notebooks and sending home the old pages, making room for new pages. We will be writing home as often as possible. Please be sure to check for messages every day and try to write a message in response, on the back of your child's message or on a separate page. It is very important to the children! Thank you!

Throughout the second half of the school year, a couple of additional reminder letters were sent. In this way, and also through parent-teacher conferences, families were frequently encouraged not to let their participation wane, though few families needed such encouragement once they recognized how much the children valued their replies and how the Family Message Journals were helping children grow as writers and learners—they saw daily evidence of progress. Children, too, can be given the responsibility for reminding their families to reply daily. In the upper grades, seeking a reply may be considered one part of students' homework, with the proviso, of course, that no child can be held accountable for a family's refusal to participate.

Since the year I studied Family Message Journals, the two first-grade teachers have decided to use premade booklets of paper as journals in lieu of loose-leaf placed in a binder. They feel this will "help us keep track of messages" for assessment purposes and discourage the loss and removal of messages from binders. Dina explained that while no child has ever lost a binder, some families have regularly removed messages they particularly liked, leaving her frustrated when searching for particular messages or sets of messages she wished to highlight in a family conference, add to the child's portfolio, or use for evaluation.

4 Writing for a Purpose: Writing as a Tool Across the Curriculum

Date: 5/2/97

Dear Family
We went to the
venchen cenvenchon
and did you know
if you had the
garbage in your
garage and you s...

page 1

the garbage thruck
comming down the
road and you had
part of a pipe or
toob that has a
round hole inside it
and it went all
the way to the
garbage you could
put the garbage
in the toob or

page 2

pipe and it would
go into the garage
then the garbage
can and you wold
have all the gar-
bage in the garba-
ge can when the
garbage truck com-
es and then you
could take it out-
side and you won't

page 3

have a full garbage
can and it won't
over flow and you
can always use it
when you forget to
take it out and to
put all of your gar-
bage in it so you
won't have to hurry
so much and that
will be good won't it

page 4

continued on next page

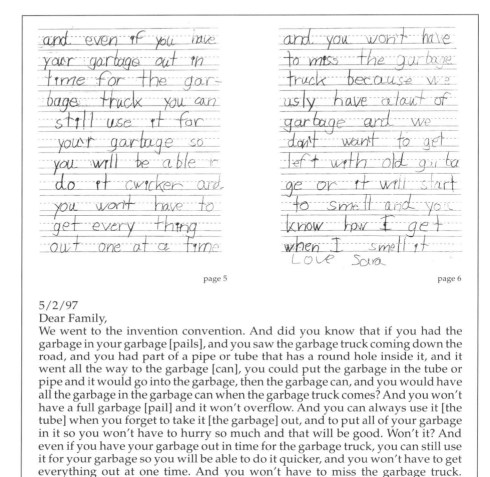

page 5   page 6

5/2/97
Dear Family,
We went to the invention convention. And did you know that if you had the garbage in your garbage [pails], and you saw the garbage truck coming down the road, and you had part of a pipe or tube that has a round hole inside it, and it went all the way to the garbage [can], you could put the garbage in the tube or pipe and it would go into the garbage, then the garbage can, and you would have all the garbage in the garbage can when the garbage truck comes? And you won't have a full garbage [pail] and it won't overflow. And you can always use it [the tube] when you forget to take it [the garbage] out, and to put all of your garbage in it so you won't have to hurry so much and that will be good. Won't it? And even if you have your garbage out in time for the garbage truck, you can still use it for your garbage so you will be able to do it quicker, and you won't have to get everything out at one time. And you won't have to miss the garbage truck. Because we usually have a lot of garbage and we don't want to get left with old garbage or it will start to smell. And you know how I get when I smell it.
Love,
Sara

Figure 4.1. Sara's "garbage invention" message reflects the way in which the Family Message Journal is a tool for learning, thinking, and self-expression.

After visiting the "Invention Convention" in her school's gymnasium, where inventions dreamed up by fifth graders were exhibited, every child in Sara's first-grade class wrote a message about this special activity. Sara's lengthy message (six double-sided 8 x 10 pages in her journal) exemplifies a number of the purposes that Family Message Journal writing can serve for children (see Figure 4.1). The journal is simultaneously a tool for learning, thinking, and self-expression. A close look at how these purposes take shape reveals the interface between student ownership and teacher control of topic and sometimes genre. First, writing after the visit encouraged Sara and her classmates to *take stock* of what they had learned through the exhibits. Each child was free to write about what stood out for him or her; flexibility within the assigned topic allowed each student to find an individual point of interest. Further, writing about the garbage tube exhibit helped Sara *remember* an invention she was eager to propose to her family, while also forcing her to *develop her idea* of exactly how it would work within her family's garbage disposal routine. In order to argue for the idea, she used writing to *recall* that her family sometimes rushes at the last minute to get all of the indoor garbage into the outdoor garbage can for pickup on garbage day each week. She enjoyed considering how the invention might change this situation, saving time and energy. Finally, Sara's message allowed her to *connect new information* about the invention *to what she already knows* about garbage disposal and its problems, and to *express her own feelings* about the distasteful odor of old garbage.

This message about the Invention Convention was written at the beginning of May. But throughout the school year, Sara and her classmates had been discovering, through the Family Message Journal, that writing serves important purposes—it helps us to remember, to make sense of new information and ideas, and to recognize, develop, and share thoughts on a topic. And because Family Message Journals are directly linked to the curriculum and related school experiences (like the Invention Convention), the messages cover a wide range of topics. This range shows children that they can write about anything and that writing is a powerful tool for thinking and communicating ideas to others, regardless of the topic.

Purposes for Writing

In looking at Sara's message about how to solve garbage disposal problems, I have identified a number of specific purposes for children's Family Message Journal writing that are related to the larger goals of thinking and communicating through writing. These purposes were identified through constant comparative analysis of all the children's messages in a search for patterns. These emergent patterns led to a categorization system that accurately represented how messages were used and that accounted for all of the messages and their purposes

(Glaser & Strauss, 1967). Closely exploring these purposes helped me develop a better understanding of what children were learning about how writing can serve their needs. These purposes include the following:

1. taking stock of new information
2. remembering responsibilities and requests
3. generating and developing ideas
4. connecting new information to the known
5. expressing personal feelings or wishes
6. recalling or savoring an experience

This list is not exhaustive—it focuses only on purposes related to writing as a tool for learning, thinking, and self-expression—but it provides a useful framework of categories for thinking about Family Message Journal entries. To illuminate the framework, this chapter focuses on examples of each category. In fact, like Sara's, many messages involved multiple purposes and thus fell into more than one of the categories listed.

Taking Stock of New Information

Family Message Journal assignments frequently asked children to reflect on a school activity by taking stock of what they had learned. This type of assignment allows teachers to focus children's attention on important learning experiences and content and requires the children *to think about* what they found out. Writing helps them come to know, or discover, what they have learned. A key difference here, however, in comparison with writing for themselves or to show a teacher what they know, is that the writing is undertaken not only as a thinking exercise but also to share school learning with family members. I come back to this point in greater detail in the next chapter, but for now it is important to point out that this situation makes it likely that children will think harder and try to tell as much as they can in as interesting a way as possible; they have readers to impress whose opinions they care about. A good example is Kyle's message about spiders, included in Chapter 3. He recorded many facts but tried to give them an interesting twist as well with his joke about spiders that suck blood being "vampires."

Other messages reviewing facts children had learned also communicated excitement and interest. In a unit on winter, the first graders investigated snowflakes outdoors in a snow shower, as Maryanne related:

january 24, 1997
Wow Mommy,
Today in the mornning we went out side and investegaited snow
flaicks. Eatch one was difrent eatch one had six sids it was so
mutch fun I think I will do it at home
    Love, Maryanne

Maryanne seems eager not only to share what she learned but also to kindle her mother's interest in the topic. Messages like this, with a written commitment to "try it at home" or "show you at home," commonly followed discovery experiences in which children were asked to observe natural objects and record in a message what they had learned. I suspect their enthusiasm about their discoveries is, at least in part, a result of being able to share their new knowledge with others.

A similar investigation into apples involved looking closely at what is inside the fruit in order to describe it in writing:

5/21/97
Dear Family
    I cut my apple open and I had two seeds in myn they were
kind of sllipery and brown and shaped like a raindrop . . . and
after I found the seeds I cut it the right way. I didn't even know I
was and I found the star Love Sara

By recording information in an accurate and thorough manner, children discovered the potential for writing to help them remember exactly what they had discovered. Such messages are the beginning of scientific writing. At the same time, these messages communicated children's interest in their topics and excitement about what they had learned. They were writing about what "grabbed" them in their own observations and discoveries, and this personal quality gave their factual writing voice. Just as they were practicing writing like a scientist or researcher, they were also experimenting with a key component of the most captivating nonfiction writing—the author's ability to communicate genuine interest in the subject.

Another example of a message in which a child took stock of her learning comes from a brief unit on potatoes in which children not only read fact and fiction about potatoes but also investigated many types and compared their texture, color, shape, weight, and "eyes." Sara wrote:

3/25/97
Dear Mom Dad and Rosa
Potato plants grow 20 to 40 inches, and they like to grow in sandy
soil. And the potato's eyes are where new potatoes grow. And
one potato plant can make 20 potatoes.
    Love, Sara

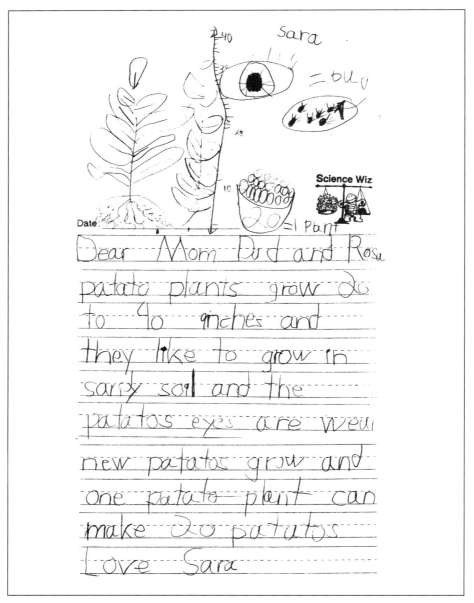

Figure 4.2. Journal entries allow children to record new information, thereby improving their chances of remembering what they learned.

Here, as in many messages, a whimsical drawing that represents facts visually accompanied the message (see Figure 4.2).

Maryanne also chose to use drawings to reinforce the information she shared about sharks (see Figure 4.3):

> February 3, 1997
> Dear Mom + Dad
> I learned that whale sharks don't eat people. Sharks only attack when they are mad or hungry. Baby sharks are called pups. Sharks can see in the dark. Sharks' eyes sometimes glow in the dark.
> Love Maryanne

Her mad shark is about to eat a person who is saying "I'm ded," but her illustration of a larger shark eating a person has a big X across it to show that this normally does not occur.

Maryanne's lengthy message about sharks was written halfway through the school year. At the beginning of the year, when expressing themselves in writing was still a time-consuming challenge, many children wrote only one fact they remembered on a topic—that which was of greatest interest or salience for them. An early October message was related to reading and discussion about the legendary figure Johnny Appleseed. Sara wrote:

> 10/4/96
> Dear Mommy PAPA Rosa
>   johnny Appleseed has a pet wuf [wolf] love.Sara

She said later that she was fascinated by the idea of a tame wolf and thought Johnny Appleseed must have been very brave to train the wild animal. Despite the brevity of her message, she had given the topic a lot of thought.

Kristen did not record any specific information about Johnny Appleseed:

> 10/4/96
> Hi mom I jesd lrd a bowt Johnny Appleseed
> Kristen

Nevertheless, her message opened up the possibility of a conversation with her family in which she could take stock of what she had learned.

At this early point in the year, many children can express more orally than in writing, and family members are often a much more attentive, encouraging audience than a single teacher can be for twenty-five children, *all* eager to talk about what they have learned and what

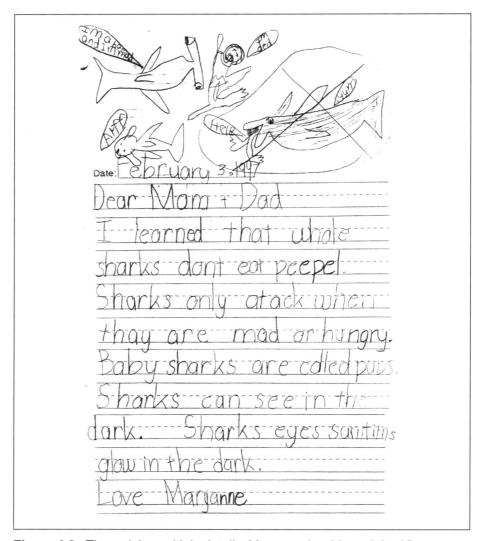

Figure 4.3. Through its multiple details, Maryanne's midyear "shark" message reflects the depth of her knowledge.

they are thinking. Family Message Journals start conversations in which even more information than that which is written down is remembered, shared, and thereby reviewed by children.

Remembering Responsibilities and Requests

Following taking stock of learning, the most frequent purpose for children's messages was to help them remember something they were expected to do or wanted a parent to help them do. This is a powerful purpose for writing that children told me they appreciated because "I might forget if I didn't write it down." Writing to remember is also a purpose they will be able to use to their advantage throughout their lives.

When the first graders were planning to make a theme-related snack at school, they were instructed to use their messages to inform parents:

> Dear Family we will be making a snack at school
> I do not need to bring a snack tomorrow Love Sara

Such assignments helped the children become aware that writing is a useful tool for remembering information they need to convey but are likely to forget otherwise.

Later in the year, children were expected to include more information in such messages and to ask for specific things they needed:

> 6/4/97
> Dear Family
> remeber to give me my snack for the bus ride and I need a good snack and a juice because we will not have lunch till 1:30 Late Lunch
> Love Sara

Sara knew the information she had to share about her field trip was important, and she worked to remember everything she thought needed to be conveyed.

Kristen's message on the same topic demonstrates how assigned entries nevertheless invited children to choose their own ways of expressing information and to select the information they viewed as most important. Kristen reminded her family not only about the need for a snack (most important of all) but also about the fact that she needed to decide immediately if she was going to buy or bring lunch on the day of the field trip:

> 6/4/97
> Dear family,
> if I'm bying for The feildtrip I need the money tomorrow if I'm Bringing Lunch I have to have Juice with it ok
> Iporton of all I need a good snack beacuse We won't eat lunch intill 1:30 Love Kristen

Other messages helped children remember things they wanted to do at home with family members. For example, after her class discussed cardinal-spotting as a sign of winter, Maryanne wrote:

January 14, 1997
Stop, Look, Listen Mommy,
The cardinals did not go south for the winter. We can look for the
bright red birds and listen for the sweet songs. Love Maryanne

This message brought about a winter walk by Maryanne and her
mother to look for cardinals. Similar messages resulted in other children
remembering to look at home for animals and other signs of winter they
had learned about in school. Writing these messages helped children
not only to remember but also to recognize how school learning could
be connected to their lives outside of school.

Family Message Journals also teach children that writing can help
them remember their own responsibilities. In Dina's and Karen's first-
grade classrooms, show-and-tell is usually related to the weekly or
monthly theme. Children are asked to find or create objects related to
current units of study that they present to their classmates orally. A
number of messages early in the year related to the week's show-and-
tell theme and served as personal reminders as well as communications
with family:

11/22/96
gobble gobble
Show and tell next week is a drawing of Thanksgiving
    Love Sara

Later in the year, messages generally required more extended writing,
and show-and-tell themes were communicated in the children's weekly
newsletter for families. Children did continue to use messages to
remember larger homework projects, however.

Generating and Developing Ideas

Writing is a powerful tool for finding out what we think and developing
our thoughts. Family Message Journal entries often involved writing to
generate ideas. One example is messages which asked children to
identify signs that a new season had begun. Through writing, Maryanne
generated ideas about signs of winter:

Brrrrr Mom and dad
I can tell it is winter!
1. The rabits fure turnes white. 2. It turnes dark at 5:00 pm! 3. The
birds fly south. 4. You can go skaiting
Love Maryanne

Kyle's message on the same topic reflected his thinking:

dear, Dad, winter, is Here, people, are, plowing los, ov, Street, and,
People, are, sledigng, and people are in thear Hous Love Kyle

Comparing these two messages, and those of other children who wrote about fire in the fireplace, professional winter sports they enjoy watching, frozen ponds, and putting birdseed out for hungry birds who don't migrate, shows that all of the children had to think about what stood out for them as signs of winter while learning that the process of writing itself can actually provoke thinking, eliciting ideas on a topic, as in brainstorming.

Children also used messages to *develop* ideas. One such message grew out of a mid-May class discussion. The first graders had talked about ways to block distractions when they were trying to focus on listening or on their independent work. Then they used their messages to figure out how and when they might implement the teacher's suggestion of trying to "put up an invisible wall" between themselves and the distraction:

> 5/12/97
> Dear Family
> Sometimes people are talking at work time and you can't get you're work dun. And sometimes you have to ask you're teacher to help. But you don't need to ask you're teacher you can put up you're invisible wall and they might stop.
>   Love
>   Sara

Through writing, Sara developed an alternative to her typical reaction to distractions—losing her focus and telling the teacher. Writing about what she could do instead helped her to consciously develop a strategy she could use independently to maintain attention to her work.

Their message assignments also helped children recognize that writing can be a tool for planning or developing a course of action on paper. Maryanne, who was anxiously awaiting a big snowstorm, prepared by writing directions for making a snowman. This message was part of a class unit on winter and focused on things children liked to do in this snowy season:

> 1. Roll a big snowball.
> 2. Roll a meedeam.
> 3. Roll the smallest snowball.
> 4. Put two rosks on the small snowball.
> 5. Put a carot wher the nose should be.
> 6. Put rasens for a mowth.

Although she did not explicitly address this message to her family, as it was really an example of writing to herself to plan, Maryanne's family did write back a sympathetic reply about how much they knew Maryanne was longing for snow.

Another example of a message used to develop plans *was* addressed to Maryanne's family because it involved something they regulated—inviting a friend to visit her house:

> March 14, 1997
> Dear Mommy and Daddy
> I can't wait till tomorro. Maby Debbi can come over oh" I'm so exited I can't wait! We will wach my new move [movie] Lassie best friends are forever
> we evin might draw Lassie oh how fun and we will play lassie to.
> I still cant wait. We will do all thoughs things tomorro.
>   Love, Maryanne

Maryanne used her teacher's invitation to write about her weekend plans to consider what she would like to do when her friend Debbi visited.

Kyle also planned what would happen on the day parents were invited to school for a cafeteria lunch:

> 3/12/97
> Dear Mom isint great you are going meat all my friens and you can go on the vacation and it's on friday and we will have a good time and yll see all the class rooms like Mrs. Willnsky and Mrs. LuBlake are cafateereea and There are flags My favrit is china
> Love Kyle

Kyle wrote this message the day before his mother's school visit in order to think through some of the things he wanted her to see. Although the assignment was simply to remind parents that they were invited for a school lunch, he recognized that developing a written plan would help him make sure the visit went as he wished.

Connecting New Information to the Known

Learning begins with the knowledge we bring to a subject. As Watson and Young (1986) explain, learning is a process in which "students . . . forge links between new knowledge and their previous understanding" (p. 126). Children must connect new information to what they know and believe in order to make sense of it, and writing can invite them to express what they know and to think about how it relates to a new topic or concept.

Some messages reflect a relatively simple process of finding something familiar in a topic that allowed children to ground new information by constructing or becoming aware of connections to it. For example, after a series of lessons on Native American culture and lifestyles, the first graders were asked to write about what they had learned. A cornbread lover, Sara wrote:

> 11/27/96
> Pop Mom Dad and Rosa
> DiD You no the nativ ameirikins mad Korn Bired Love Sara

A seemingly straightforward bit of information was of great interest to Sara because she enjoyed making cornbread with her mother and eating it warm from the oven. This home experience provided a connection between *her* life and the new information she was learning in school. Writing in her Family Message Journal helped her make that connection.

Maryanne's message on the topic of Native Americans, an example from Chapter 3, likewise shows her using her message to relate new information to what she knows and how she lives. She marveled that Native Americans did not have large grocery stores like the Shaw's chain where her family shops but instead had to grow or hunt for their food themselves.

Similarly, Kyle was able to remember what he had learned during a February history discussion of Presidents George Washington and Abraham Lincoln because he formed and wrote about a connection to his baby sister Elizabeth's name:

> They Had a Big war The North vrst [versus] The south are catry [country] was The north
> Befor They Had kings and sam [some] queens
> spane had a king
> inglid [England] Had a king   and you know wat
> ingland had a queen cald queen alizaBeth like are baby
> love kyle

Another example of messages helping children ground new information in what they already know and think comes from very early in the school year. The first-grade classes were involved in a study of apples, including their significance as a symbol of autumn and their role in folklore, as exemplified by characters such as Johnny Appleseed. The apple-related messages discussed earlier in this chapter grew out of this unit. Before the students began studying apples, their teachers asked them to write messages expressing their ideas about the topic. Several messages reflect how students used writing to bring out and record their own thoughts as they launched into their study of apples. Kristen wrote:

Dear Family
I think apples are sweet Love Kristen

Maryanne also likes apples—raw—because she likes the juice:

October 2, 1996
Hi Mom + DAD
I lik Ro APPLES Kos i Lik the joos
Love, Maryanne

The topic also made Maryanne think of her past apple-picking experiences at Andrew's house. In another message, she wrote:

September 30, 1996
Hello Mommy and DAddy
WeN CEN WE GO APPLE PEKING AT ANDROOS HOES
LOVE Maryanne

This type of writing to "get into" a topic invites children to work from what they know and believe and feel, paving the way for learning by giving them a foundation on which to build.

Children can also use Family Message Journals to make sense of events and of stories they read in terms of their own experiences. When the first graders were asked to respond to the story *An Extraordinary Egg* (Lionni, 1994) by writing about their favorite characters, Maryanne made sense of her favorite character Jessica's behavior in terms of her own friend's behavior:

April 10 97
Jessicka reminds me of one of my frends Marissa she brags about evrething she finds and makes and things Like that. That is why she's not my best frend. Some times she drivs me crazy! But she's still a good frend even thogh she sometims makes me mad.
Maryanne

It was not until she actually wrote this response that Maryanne made the connection, or even thought consciously about who was her favorite character in the story and why. By writing she revealed her thoughts to herself and made sense of her reactions.

After learning that as part of her town's two hundredth birthday there would be a parade and fireworks, Sara wrote:

6/3/97
Dear Family
We made a picture about [our town's] birthday we made fireworks and floats and people in a band and little stands to sell things and houses and people looking out windows and cheere leaders and if you had fireworks in yor picture it would be better

> if it were night and a light moon and know clouds so you could
> see the fireworks
>   Love Sara

As she wrote, she used her previous knowledge of events such as parades and fireworks to figure out that unlike the parade, which would be best scheduled during daylight hours for the benefit of spectators, the fireworks would be better held at night, preferably on a cloudless night. This message is also a good example of how teachers can integrate all subject areas into the Family Message Journal, including "specials" such as art, for which they are not primarily responsible. The picture Sara described was created during art period, with the school's art teacher, as part of a schoolwide focus on local history.

As the task of writing became easier for the children and their messages grew longer over the course of the year, *many* entries reflected the kind of thinking on paper that is evident in some of the preceding examples. When children can and do continue writing beyond the basic "We made a picture of [our town's] birthday" or "Jessica reminds me of my frend Marissa," they naturally begin to use their messages to think more about their topics and look for connections to what they know. This is one reason, as noted in Chapter 3, teachers should encourage children to write more, perhaps by asking, "What else could you write about that?" rather than always accept the children's first efforts as complete. Of course, some children enjoy writing more than others and will keep on independently, but all children benefit at times from encouragement to "tell your family more."

Expressing Personal Feelings or Wishes

As the preceding examples illustrate, all of the children's writing expressed their particular ideas or their own learning related to a topic. Yet some of their messages focused specifically on recording their personal imaginings and helped them see that writing can be used to capture and share feelings and wishes. For example, on the hundredth day of school, as teachers were trying to develop the mathematical concept of how one hundred of some objects may seem like a lot more than one hundred of others, the children were asked to imagine what they would do if they had one hundred dollars. Sara wrote of her wishes:

> 2/10/97
> Dear Mom Dad and Rosa
> if I had 100 dolirs I wud spend it on a new wawch [watch] and
> toys and gooliry [jewelry] and that is what I wud do
>   Love Sara

Messages related to reading also invited the expression of personal feelings. Sometimes Dina and Karen encouraged personal response to a book by asking the children to write about their favorite characters. In a previous example, Maryanne compared her favorite character, Jessica in *An Extraordinary Egg* (Lionni, 1994), to a particular friend. Taking a different approach to the favorite character assignment, Kristen wrote about her personal feelings for Charlotte in *Charlotte's Web* (White, 1952) as if she knew the spider:

> 5/30/97
> Charlat is a good writer and she is cined [kind]
> she is a good freind to Wilber
> she is sweet
> and she is nise
> She is very helpfule I like her
> Kristen

Being asked to write such messages helped children recognize that expressing their personal feelings for characters is a valid way to respond to a book. Further, Kristen demonstrated the critical ability to support her feelings with reasons, listing some of Charlotte's special qualities.

Another message which invited children to record their personal ideas and feelings was related to an early January unit on dental health coordinated with the school's health teacher. The class had discussed how to care for one's teeth and normal stages of dental development, including loss and growth of teeth. The first graders were in the process of losing their first teeth. Still believers, many wondered about the tooth fairy's appearance and mode of carrying out her job of collecting "baby" teeth from under sleeping children's pillows and leaving a surprise in their place. Recognizing the children's great interest, their teachers invited them to write a message about what the tooth fairy looks like. Like her classmates, Sara took very seriously the job of expressing her personal vision of extreme beauty:

> Tooth mom dad and Rosa
> I thingk the tooth fary has a pink Gres [dress] and pink soes
> [shoes]and brown hair
> Love Sara

A final example of children using writing to express their personal ideas comes from a March unit on wind and weather. The class had discussed how wind helps people but can also be destructive. Maryanne wrote:

March 13, 1997
Dear Family The wind isn't allways horible it can help you dry the wash. It is very usefull it mouvs the wether. if we didn't have wind we'd all ways have the same wether now that would be boring
Love, Maryanne

While sharing some of what she had learned, Maryanne also shared her personal appreciation for changes in the weather, expressing how she would feel if there were no wind.

Recalling or Savoring an Experience

Writing can be a wonderful tool for remembering and reliving a significant experience. In March the school had a Pajama Day; children, teachers, and the principal wore pajamas to school and brought the stuffed animals they slept with. The first graders delighted in the unusual spectacle of pajamas in school and the opportunity to keep stuffed animals on their desks all day long. Maryanne used her message journal to recall the day for herself as well as to inform her family:

Dear Mom + Dad Pujama day was fun Chops [Beanie Baby stuffed animal] got to stay at my seat all day long she behaved herself very well. The teacher had funny pujamas cat in the hat pujamas Molly had bunny pujamas Debbi had color pujamas and I wore my strawberry pujamas. Love, Maryanne

Writing on this topic allowed Maryanne to savor the experience.

Other messages invited children to recall home experiences, such as what they had done on a day when school was closed unexpectedly due to a snowstorm. Kyle wrote the following message after several consecutive days of school cancellations during which his mother had to work:

4/7/97
Dear Mom the storm was funn I went sleding I had a friend over we played super Mareao and then we played hockey then we jumped in the ball pit then we watched television then we went sleding. The next day we went to the movie with my casn [cousin] his names joey to see the sixth man one part was funny when harr the hosky tail on the seesaw love Kyle

Entries focusing on reading also sometimes invited the children to recall a text they had enjoyed. The way in which the teachers framed such message assignments shaped what and how children wrote. When assignments asked children to discuss their reactions or feelings about a book or to write about their favorite characters, they guided children to express personal feelings. But when they asked children to "tell what happened in the book" or "tell what the book is about," they encouraged them to recall the plot or information presented. An example of such a message comes from Sara's journal. She wrote an entry which allowed her to recall and savor her pleasure in the amusing plot and satisfying resolution of the story *Singing Sam* (Bulla, 1989). Sam, a dog, runs away from his cruel owner, Rob, who is glad to see him go. Kind Amy finds runaway Sam, he learns to sing along as she plays the piano, and he is featured on a television show. Rob sees the show and demands return of his now-famous dog, but in the end Rob gives the dog back to Amy when Sam refuses to perform for an owner who doesn't really care for him. Sara recalled:

> Singing Sam ran away and a girl found him in her yard She teecht him how to sing this dog beelogde [belonged] to the boy named Rob. the girls name wus Amy She went on TV and the [then] Rob wawntid him ugen then Rob took him bak then he gayv him to the girl named Amy. Love Sara

Sara explained orally to her family that she was very happy with the outcome of the story—Rob had not been nice to Sam *or* fair to Amy.

Finally, teachers can invite children to use their Family Message Journals to recall past experiences and discover how, through writing, they can remember and savor the details of even distant events and times in their lives. Dina Carolan and Karen Wilensky plan a number of end-of-year messages which ask children to look back at the first-grade experience. An example of one of these messages, Kristen's nostalgic poem "My first grade book," is included in Chapter 3. Another message assignment asked children to write about an experience from the autumn that they wanted to relive. In early June Sara wrote:

> 6/1/97
> Dear Family
> remember when we made turcees [turkeys] at thancksgiving and we went to virmont at thanksgiving with you and we had a tircky and we went to virmont on Wednesday and came back on Sunday afternoon after lunch and the leaves were all diffrent colors it was audunm and it was cool and I raked leaves in a pile and jumped in them and it is still good to rake things in to a pile like the tree pollen that fell now and I want to rake it
> Love Sara

Writing this message enabled Sara to savor a relatively distant experience.

Sharing Messages

As discussed in Chapter 3, having children share their messages with classmates by reading them aloud is a valuable learning strategy. The messages included as examples throughout this chapter show that although children were writing on the same assigned topics, they came at these topics in unique ways and often remembered and highlighted very different information. Sharing their messages expanded children's learning as peers presented new information or connections or reminded classmates of forgotten facts. Sharing also modeled various perspectives from which one can write about a topic and demonstrated ways of writing with voice and energy. Each day the first-grade teachers selected several children, giving them a turn to read their journal entries aloud. The teachers rotated students regularly but also tried to select systematically those whose messages provided particularly good examples of ways of using writing as a tool or of expressing ideas in writing. Sharing could then include explicit discussion of aspects the teachers wished to highlight in the shared entries.

The Teacher's Role Revisited

The children's writing included in this chapter should help further elucidate the teacher's role in designing journal entry assignments that make the activity beneficial in terms of learning new information and developing varied ways of using writing.

Through the examples in this chapter I have tried to show how Family Message Journals can be used to help children see the potential of writing as a purposeful tool for learning, thinking, and self-expression. Looking across journal entries—the many focused on aspects of the winter season, for example—can also help students discover how information and ideas are connected thematically and recognize diverse ways of presenting related information or ideas.

The messages in this chapter also show how the potential power of writing is best tapped when teachers carefully plan the topics and types of messages children will be asked to write daily, rather than leaving this to chance or last-minute planning. Careful planning—with room for flexibility, of course—can ensure that children learn a variety of purposes for writing and develop a general sense of how it can help them academically and benefit them personally to express ideas in writing.

Planning coexisted with flexibility in Dina's and Karen's classrooms. For example, the teachers planned for children to use Family Message Journals regularly to recall and report on the many hands-on science experiments they conducted. Students' enthusiasm for such entries, however (apparently growing out of their excitement about the activity itself), resulted in their teachers assigning them more such entries than they might have with a different group of children. Sometimes a popular message topic led to related message assignments, as when the children expressed so much interest in learning and writing about optical illusions that they wrote multiple messages, explaining not only their own experiments, as their teachers had planned, but also what makes optical illusions occur, how they are used in magic shows, and how to make some "magic" at home.

Moreover, although topic assignments were carefully considered, the teachers left message topics open enough to allow children to find ways of expressing what mattered most to them about a topic. And, as is evident from the children's messages included here, their teachers gave careful thought to framing topics in engaging ways. The messages reflect children's involvement in the topics and sense of empowerment as they deliver information to their family members.

5 Writing for an Audience: The Functions of Children's Messages

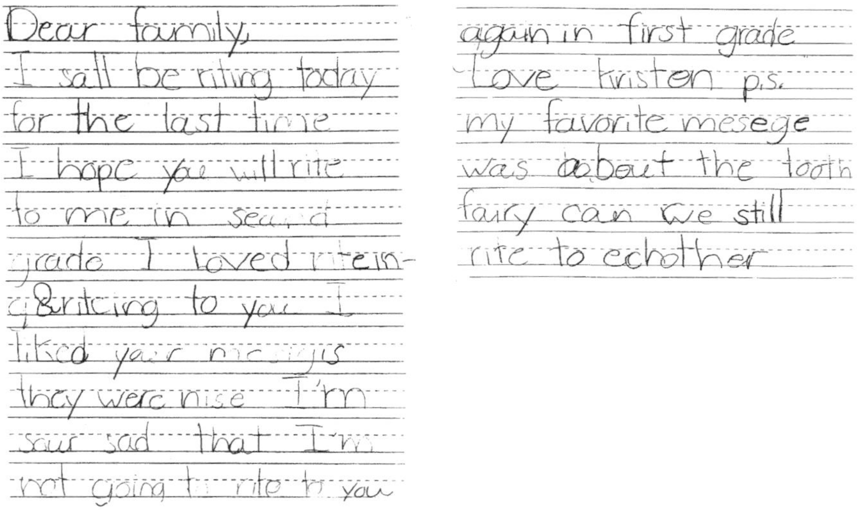

Dear Family,
    I shall be writing today for the last time. I hope you will write to me in second grade. I loved writing & writing to you. I liked your messages. They were nice. I'm so sad that I'm not going to write to you again in first grade. Love, Kristen
    P.S. My favorite message was about the tooth fairy. Can we still write to each other?

Figure 5.1. Kristin's final first-grade journal entry reveals the value students place on Family Message Journal correspondence.

In this chapter, I use a lens different from that in Chapter 4 to explore Family Message Journal entries. Here I focus on the messages' *functions*—how the first graders used their journals to communicate with and influence their families. Like Kristen's entry in Figure 5.1, many of the children's messages reveal that the journals became a significant aspect of their relationships with their families—a way to interact with them on a daily basis around school-related topics. Kristen's message exemplifies the value children placed on this interaction. She indicates how much she enjoyed the written communication, hopes it will continue in second grade, and even recalls a favorite message written five months earlier. Her first sentence, one of many possible openings her class had discussed for this final message, is modeled after the words of Charlotte, the spider, in E. B. White's (1952) *Charlotte's Web,* spoken before spinning a final message in her web. Dina Carolan had recently read aloud this classic story to Kristen and her classmates, and they agreed that both the formality of and the sadness in Charlotte's words were a fitting way to wrap up the journal writing which had meant so much to them.

Message Functions

In order to look at the functions of the children's writing vis-à-vis their audience—their families—I have drawn on Halliday's (1975) category system for the functions of oral language, adapting this system to children's written messages. The adaptation makes sense because Halliday's categories fit so well when describing how the children's messages functioned. In fact, Halliday's categories more accurately describe and encompass the many functions than do category systems developed specifically for written language. This close fit may reflect the fact that the messages were similar to oral language in their conversational, interactive, and immediately pragmatic nature. They were (like talk) used by the first graders to act on the world and to get things done in the context of their immediate relationships with family members. The children's messages served the following purposes:

1. to inform families (like Informative Language in Halliday's framework)

2. to regulate families' behavior (like Regulatory Language in Halliday's framework)

3. to get things from families (like Persuasive Language in Halliday's framework)

4. to interact with families (like Interactional Language in Halliday's framework)

5. to share personal ideas and feelings with families (like Personal Language in Halliday's framework)

6. to create an imagined textual experience for families (like Imaginative Language in Halliday's framework)

7. to figure things out through communication with families (like Heuristic Language in Halliday's framework)

This chapter explores multiple Family Message Journal entries exemplifying each of these categories; keep in mind, however, that any category system is somewhat artificial. While serving as a useful heuristic for examining the first graders' messages, the categories are not always discrete. Some messages integrate multiple functions. For example, personal feelings about owls may be included in an informative entry about owls, which might also involve an attempt to figure out why owls are considered wise in popular folklore. Nevertheless, for the sake of clarity and explanatory power, I will look at each category separately.

Informing Families

Family Message Journal assignments frequently invited the first graders to inform families about information the children thought their families did not know, and often they were right. For example, Sara had learned some information about owls that surprised her family:

> 2/25/97
> Whoo whoo Family,
> owls mite eat mice, fish, snakes, rabbits, and even skunks! Do you know why owl does not mind the smell of skunks? I do

Sara's suggestion that she knows something her family does not was typical in the children's entries. In talking about this entry at home, she answered her own question orally and enlightened her family.

Family Message Journals positioned children as the "experts" who had important facts to share. Kyle's message, written as part of a March unit on wind, exemplifies his sense of expertise as he begins "I know when hurricanes come":

> Yipe Mom and Dad I know when Hurkans come in the late summer you need wind if we did't have wind we would't have anee kites and we would not have saleBoat we would't Be cool we would Be Hot for rest av are life

Late in the school year when studying local history, the first graders learned about the soldier after whom their school had been named. Asked to write about this lesson, Maryanne shared her knowledge, listing the facts she had learned and making some interesting personal connections to these facts:

> May 23, 1997
> Dear Mommy, L.T. [school's name] was a very important solgere. Hear are a few facts I know about him. 1. He died on November 29 that is my birthday! 2. Mrs. Wilensky went to school with Mr. [soldier's name]. She was in first grade when he was in sixth grade.

    3. He was shot when he was 22. 4. He was born on April 23. Inter-
esting facts, huy? Do you know that Greg's dad was in the army
Love, Maryanne

Like Maryanne's "Interesting facts, huh?," the children's rhetorical questions often revealed their sense of having something engaging to share.

    Even when their information was more widely known, children's
messages reflected their feeling of empowerment at being able to "test"
their families' knowledge:

    11/26/96
    Dear Mom Did you know The Pilgrims, sleard [sailed] on The
    May Flower Did you know that?
    Love Kristen

Kristen's "Did you know that?" reads like a challenge to match her
knowledge. Her mother obliged, replying with information about
where the Pilgrims landed—nearby Plymouth, Massachusetts.

    Families' replies often reinforced the first graders' sense of being
bearers of genuinely new information. After engaging in a number of
scientific experiments about vision and how the eyes play tricks on us,
Maryanne wrote:

    November 12, 1996
    Abracadabra Mommy
    Science is magic.
    I can show you a few good trickx
    Would you like that? yes no
    Surcol your ansur

In her reply to this message, after being shown the "tricks," Maryanne's
mother confirmed that she had learned something new from her
daughter:

    Nov. 13, 1996
    Hi Maryanne!
        Thank you very much for showing us the science tricks. It
    was fun. I never knew I had a hole in my hand or hot dog on my
    fingers.
        Science is fun!
                            Love
                               Mommy

Reply messages frequently let the children know that their messages
were having an effect—families were learning from the children and
found it interesting.

Regulating Families' Behavior

Children's behavior is so often regulated by adults that it must be empowering for them to find that they can sometimes turn the tables. The first graders discovered they could use writing to tell their families to do something and that it often worked. Families allowed the messages to shape their behavior.

Some of the children's messages were simple reminders to families to do something that was required.

> Dear Family
> We are going on a fieldtrip!!!! I need to bring $3.00 by May 29 I can bring a snack to eat on the bus.
> Love, Sara

Sara's message got her family's attention, and she was given three dollars to bring to school the next day.

Children's regulatory messages were sometimes phrased indirectly or as suggestions, but they were nevertheless intended to make family members do something. Following a lesson on recycling, Sara wanted her family to reuse not only the back side of used paper, as they already did, but also to keep paper that had any blank spaces on either side and add to those until the paper was completely full:

> Dear Family
> We can use a peas of paper and draw on the back and add to the old ones Love Sara

Other regulatory messages were more directive. Maryanne wanted to make sure her mother, father, and older sister would follow the cafeteria rules when they came to visit for a school lunch. She explained exactly how they should behave:

> March 12, 1997
> Dear Mom Dad and Joanna who can come to lunch tommoro? Can Mom come, can Dad come, or can Joanna come. Whoever can come I have to tell them some rools. You must stay in your seet. Rase your hand when [the cafeteria monitor] dose that means be quiet. And if you don't be quiet you go in the five minut cloub that is not good.
> Love, Maryanne

This message was effective in getting Maryanne's older sister to agree, in her reply, to come for lunch and to follow the rules so she could avoid being placed in "the five minute [time out] club"!

After a discussion of safety rules for automobile transportation, rules which integrated a series of lessons by the health teacher and a "Weekly Reader" article read with her classroom teacher, Maryanne wrote a strongly worded message to her family:

> March 17, 1997
> Buckle up!!! Mom and Dad
> Please put Me in the back seat it's the safest playse in the car. DON'T!!! drink alcohol befor driveing you Will get drunk and you might get in a car acksedent. Allways buckle Me up buckle your self up to. Dont drive when you are verry verry verry verry old. Don't drive when the wether is bad.
>   Love, Maryanne

In the reply message, her family reinforced Maryanne's power to regulate their behavior by assuring her they would follow all of these rules and pointing out that they already did obey some of them, such as buckling seat belts.

Getting Things from Families

Messages written to get things from families were similar to those written to regulate behavior, but messages written to get things involved persuading families to buy something, help with something, or consider a special request. These messages were less commandlike than regulatory messages that told families they must, or at least *should*, do something.

The first graders discovered that a written message asking for something sometimes got more attention than an oral plea, in part because family members could choose to read it at a moment when they were able to give it their complete attention and in part because the writing reflected the amount of work put into making the plea, as well as the thinking behind it. The children also found that writing helped them organize and remember all of their ideas, so they made a stronger argument for what they wanted from family members than they might have made in spontaneous oral conversation.

Early in the year, most persuasive messages were simply requests with the word *please* used to enhance the chances of success. Maryanne's message accompanying a book club order form, asking that she be allowed to order a book entitled *Mouse Paint* (Walsh, 1989), is a good example:

> September 26, 1996
> Hi
> MAY I PlEese GeT THE BooK MAWSPANTE
> LOVE, MARYANNE
> OXXOOXXOOXXOOXXOOXXO

Maryanne's row of symbolic hugs and kisses (O's and X's) could only help her cause! Such messages were common because the first-grade teachers gave the children responsibility for communicating with their families about book orders and other special opportunities and events.

Kristen took a slightly different approach to persuasion when her class was planning a special activity called spelling baseball:

> 5/20/97
> Dear family
> I need 4 words To do for spelling baseball what do you think cod be good can you help me please it will be fun Love Kristen
> 1. _____
> 2. _____
> 3. _____
> 4. _____

Kristen tried to get her family's help with generating words by arguing that it would be fun for them to participate and by giving them spaces to fill in. In other messages, she tried different approaches to getting what she wanted from her family. For example, when she wanted them to take her to see the fifth-grade play being staged at the high school, she wrote:

> 5/6/97
> Dear family,
> We are writing adout [about] Joseph's amazing Technicolor Dream Coat let's go to the play Tonight Friday may 9th saturday May 10th 7:00 at the High school I wan't to go so much to the play I'll be sad if you say no Love Kristen

In this message, she appealed to her family's compassion, saying she would be disappointed if they did not do what she had requested.

Several of the children's messages throughout the year related to science units about animals that are sometimes kept as pets. This led to a number of requests for a pet. When Kristen's class learned about newborn kittens, she wrote:

> Meow mom And dad
> a kitten stase with thier mother for 6 manths after thier born And a kitten do not open thier eyes intill thier ten monse old that's why I wont a kitten I'll die for one Love Kristen p.s But I Know I'm algec [allergic] to them Mom I Don't mind if i'm lirgeck To them I gest [just] wont one Plese Plese with a chere on top I wont one I beg you plese plese plese I wont one so much beaus they are so cyoot [cute] Plese mom I love you
> I wont a kitten so Bad if you say no I'll die But I Bet I know you wont care arent I rite you are the Best mom if you say yes so plese say yes I'll Do ene [any] Thing I promis I Bet your tirD of reDing so I'll stop

Kristen tried yet another set of strategies in this message, beginning with arousing her family's sympathy for a newborn kitten that clearly needs protection, as well as explaining just how much she wants a kitten—she would die for one. Moreover, she anticipated and tried to address her mother's potential objection that Kristen is allergic to cats, and continued her message with a common childhood plea (pretty please with a cherry on top). She also added further reasoning to support her wish—she wants a kitten because they are so cute. Trying another tactic, she attempted to arouse some guilt to further her cause, writing, "I know you won't care. Aren't I right?" Next she tried flattery—"Mom, I love you" and "You are the best mom" (but only if you agree to my request!). And, finally, she offered to reciprocate if she got what she wanted—"I'll do anything, I promise."

Like Kristen, the other first graders composed increasingly sophisticated messages to get things they wanted as the year progressed. Kristen's next message requesting a kitten focused on only one strategy of persuasion, but she developed her argument well and made the convincing and coherent case that she deserved a kitten:

> 1/16/97
> Dear mom And dad can I Have a kitten for a Pet I Will take cear [care] of her I will feed her I will woke [walk] her I will Play whith her And I will Love her I promis Love Kristen PS plees may I have a kitten

This is an organized and well-reasoned, if less passionate, message than the first one. Kristen indicated her awareness that having a pet requires time and effort, and she promised to care for a kitten if she got one.

A similar message from Sara demonstrated her awareness that she must give something to get something:

> 4/11/97
> Dear Family
> I want to get lots of books from the bookorder and I want to clean the dishes for you only if you pay me I don't cear [care] how much I get because I have lots of alouens [allowance] money but I don't mind if I can't get any how many will I get if you can buy me some I want it to be too sets of books I want the prary [prairie] ones can I they come in a pack their are nine books in the set Love Sara

In her message asking for a family contribution toward the book order, Sara also offered to work to earn money to buy some of the books she wanted, as well as to spend some of her own allowance money, earned for doing chores and for good behavior.

The children's success with messages written to get things from their families demonstrated that writing is powerful. Aside from requests for pets, only some of which were granted, nearly all of the other persuasive messages the first graders wrote were successful—whenever possible they went to the events they hoped to attend; they were permitted to order books they asked for—and their families' replies included explicit recognition of how convincing their messages were. Many of these replies indicated that it was the children's awareness that they would have to make sacrifices to get what they wanted that made families agree to their requests. For example, Sara's father replied to her book order message:

> 4/14/97
> Dear Sara
> You've made a good start earning money to help pay for the things you want to buy. I'm glad you are beginning to appreciate how much time and work it takes to have the things you want.
> Love, Papa

By writing in their Family Message Journals, the children grew increasingly skilled in convincing their families that they did have this appreciation.

Interacting with Families

Many of the first graders' Family Message Journal entries were used primarily to interact with families—to define, develop, and sustain relationships. Some of these messages focused on telling a family member what she or he meant to the child writer. Maryanne's Father's Day message is a good example:

> June 12, 1997
> Dear Daddy,
> Fathers day is coming up. You could reseve a littl somthing! You are the best dad in the world! You are Dinamic, brave, and funny.
> Love, Maryanne

Attached to this entry was a sheet of paper on which Maryanne had brainstormed special things about her father and all the words she could think of to describe him.

Other messages shared memories and feelings about activities enjoyed with a family member. Again, a good example is a message written by Maryanne to her father, a journal entry inspired by a poem her class read about walking outside and feeling the warm sun and seeing other early signs of spring (Aldis, 1968):

> February 24, 1997
> Dear Daddy - Do you Rember are nice walk on Sunday? remeber
> how I found my lost list of Bine [Beanie] Babies I wanted? It was
> fun wasent it! Love Maryanne

Sometimes the first graders were given the assignment to use
their messages to express appreciation to their families for a special
event or experience. After her birthday party, Maryanne wrote:

> December 2, 1996
> Dear Mommy + Daddy
> I in joyed my birthday. I in joyed the prezents I in joyed the cake
> and I in joyed the fun too
> Love maryanne

Kristen wrote a similar message of appreciation when Dina Carolan
invited her class to reflect on something special they had done over the
December holiday vacation and tell their families how they felt about it:

> Dear mom
> I loved the baskitball Game I thalt [thought] that bran bib [did]
> excslint And I loved Alisons houes Also I loved MicDanls
> [MacDonald's] it was fun Love Kristen

Other messages of appreciation explicitly thanked families for
something they allowed or engaged in with the first graders. Kyle wrote
to thank his mom for letting him sleep over at his cousin's house and
also told her what he had done there:

> H MoM Thaiks for leting Me go to My Ksin sleep Oaver We got
> to play on the Coputer it WaS Fun love Kyle

Sara thanked *her* family for a holiday visit to a farm:

> HaPPy new Yeer
> mom dad and Rosa i like the cows the moast and i likte the baby
> caf the moast thank you for brining me Love Sara

Families truly valued these messages of appreciation and thanks and let
the children know how much they were touched by them, reinforcing
the power of writing to maintain and enhance a relationship. These
messages also introduced the children to an important and common
form of out-of-school writing—the thank-you note—and helped them
see how influential such a note can be.

Another type of interactional message involved asking family
members for their opinions on an issue or idea, as if in a conversation:

> 1/7/97
> fary [fairy] dust mom dad and Rosa I thingk the tooth fary maks
> them [teeth] in to fary dust wut do You thingk mom and dad
> Love Sara

After offering her opinion, Sara asked her family members for their opinions on what the tooth fairy does with the teeth she collects. Similarly, Maryanne asked her family their feelings about sharing belongings:

> December 16, 1996
> Dear Mommy + Daddy
> do you like sharing your earing's? how douse sharing make you feel? do you like to share?
>   Love, Maryanne

In reply, Maryanne's mother expressed her feelings about sharing, acknowledging how it can feel to share as a child, but also explaining her feelings about sharing as an adult:

> December 16, 1996
> Dear Maryanne,
>   Yes, I like sharing. But when I was little I liked everything for myself. Now I like to share and to give. It makes me feel VERY, VERY GOOD and HAPPY. It makes me feel WARM inside!
>   Love,
>   Mommy

Maryanne's message and her mother's reply are like a conversation on paper, exemplifying how Family Message Journals can function to facilitate interaction within families and thereby maintain relationships.

Sharing Personal Ideas and Feelings with Families

Although many messages included personal feelings and ideas, the first graders' Family Message Journal entries sometimes functioned *primarily* to express their ideas and feelings to their families. Chapter 4 discussed messages in which the first graders got their ideas and feelings down on paper as a learning strategy. Here I focus on messages in which children were intent on *sharing* their ideas and feelings with family members. Some of these messages grew out of a series of lessons on becoming familiar with and conscious of our feelings and how each of us expresses them. One example is Kristen's message on feeling mad:

> 12/9/96
> Dear mom and dAd When I am mad my arms are crost And I stap [stamp] my Feet bcas [because of] my sister love kristen

Writing this message allowed her to communicate that what usually makes her mad is her older sister's behavior toward her.

Kyle also reflected on feeling angry, sharing his experience of going alone to his mother's room and quietly crying:

12/9/96
olu [Hello] DAD When I Whus Mad I Wet to My Momthers room
and be quighit [quiet] my fais [face] is cring [crying] kyle

Kyle's message is accompanied by an illustration of a child lying flat on
a bed with tears on his face.

Maryanne's message about feeling mad addresses why people
get mad. She imagined a situation which would make her mad:

October 25, 1996
Dear Mom + Dad Janet is Felling mad today Her frend was play-
ing with her dog boy was she mad   Love Maryanne

Messages like these about common emotions and how they are aroused
and handled met with sympathetic replies expressing families' understanding of how siblings and friends could make the first graders angry,
as well as acknowledgment that anger is normal:

October 25, 1996
Dear Maryanne!
     We all feel mad sometimes. But it is part of life to have feel-
ings. And it is very important to talk about your feelings.
                              I Love You!
                              Mommy

Sometimes the feelings children shared in their Family Message
Journals were more immediate than the reflections presented in the
preceding messages, which focus on past experiences with anger or
events likely to make one angry. For example, when preparing to go on
her first field trip ever, Maryanne shared a concern in her journal:

May 20, 1997
Dear Mommy, We'r having a feild-Trip. I'm a little nervis. Mrs.
Wilensky says mayby you can come. Can you come? Oh please
pritty pritty please with sugar and bunches of chocalet on top!
please! Natasha's mom is comming mayby you to can talk together
          Love Maryanne

This message is a good example of how some entries served multiple
functions. The message assignment was to inform families about the
upcoming field trip and invite chaperone volunteers. This resulted in
many persuasive messages, such as Maryanne's in which she tried to
get her mother to come on the trip. But the Family Message Journal also
allowed Maryanne to express her fears and doubts and receive needed
support and reassurance. Maryanne's mother's reply was an attempt to
help Maryanne overcome her anxiety about the trip.

In another entry, reflecting on the special, year-end athletic event called "field day," Maryanne used her Family Message Journal to communicate her displeasure with her mother's behavior:

> June 10, 1997
> Dear Mama, Today we are having popsicles. Field day was so much fun! But verry swety and hot! A verry good thing I brought my water bottle. You came late and left erly I'm not happy about it. Love, Maryanne

The journal allowed Maryanne to voice her anger and her mother to explain why she had to leave early—their new puppy was too young to stay in the hot sun for more than a short time, and there was no shade by the field.

Children also used Family Message Journals to share positive feelings. In a message in which the first graders were asked to explore their feelings about spring, Maryanne wrote:

> March 25, 1997
> Dear mom and Dad
> I prifer the wether to be nice because we'r going on vacachon in florida. I also like spring because you don't always need to ware jacet's and it get's warmer to. Spring is also the time I'm getting my ears pearst. oh I can't wait till spring. Spring is the time wen easter comes. Spring is the time wen Mommy stops working. Spring is the time the birds come back.
> Love Maryanne

Maryanne's message communicated her excitement about upcoming events which her family had arranged. She let them know how much she valued their plans.

Similarly, when invited by her teacher to write about field day, Sara used her message to share her feelings with her family and, thereby, invite them to experience the fun she had:

> Dear Family
> my favoret thing was the balloon toss and the tugawar we all shoad good sportmenship and I really like the tugawar because felicia couldn't hold on tight and I couldn't pull hard enaf [enough] and Mrs. Carolan said it looked like water skeeing and Mrs. McKay and Mrs. Carolan hid a balloon intile [until] they could drop it on Mr. Bohane and when they did it went on his neck then Mrs. Walenscie put a water balloon in Mr. Bohane's hat and when he put his hat on it went on his head every body thawt it was funny Love Sara

Writing this message allowed Sara to share her pleasure at watching her gym teacher get tricked by the first-grade teachers.

Creating an Imagined Textual Experience for Families

Though a number of Family Message Journal entries involved imagining and creating worlds or situations for the purpose of generating ideas or exploring a theme of study creatively, some entries were aimed specifically at creating an imagined textual experience *for families.* The children often sought family members' feedback before finishing these stories, which were usually written as a series of entries over two or three days. Family members provided a real audience—the children could gauge the impact of their imaginary ideas on readers who would respond. The first-grade teachers generated some story-writing assignments with this potential feedback in mind.

During a unit on mice, the first graders together brainstormed some ideas for "mouse tales" and discussed basic story structure. Then they began writing their stories as messages, accompanied by a teacher's note explaining the process and how they had worked on one story element in particular—setting (place and time). The note indicated that this was just the start; "we'll continue with the characters and plots later in the week." The beginning of Maryanne's story for her family read:

> November 5, 1996
> Dear Mom + Dad
> many years ago In a byuteeful medo ther was a mouse naemd gaby. the medo haed a . . . . . streem the streem was Verea clean weth fish

Maryanne's family responded with interest and replied that they were eager to find out what would happen to Gaby.

Two days later, Maryanne continued the story in her Family Message Journal:

> November 7, 1996
> Gaby had a frend naemd Gordana Gaby and Gordana lovd to play together taye [they] like to play gayms like tage and hide and go squeek It was fun just then tay saw a cat! you cat! thay shreekt iff that cat cachis us that wolde [would] be the ende of us quiklee thay hed [hid]

This was as far as she got until the next day. Her family's reply to this second installment indicated how successfully Maryanne had created suspense, keeping them interested in reading what would happen next. Her father even made a few predictions about what he thought might happen.

By writing an imaginary text for her family and getting their replies, Maryanne was supported in her creative efforts and provided with specific feedback on what she had done well as well as suggestions about where her story might go. In short, her family served as a skilled conference partner—just as her teacher might have. This is one example of families' abilities to serve successfully as teacher, and it is typical of the first graders' supportive, instructive experiences with Family Message Journals.

Figuring Things Out through Communication with Families

The first graders sometimes used their messages to explore ideas or ask questions of their families in an effort to solve a problem, figure out a challenge, or find out about something. Writing about science experiments for their families encouraged children to fully develop and explain their hypotheses and what they eventually found, and it allowed them to share their thinking with interested readers. In June, before conducting an experiment involving marbles on inclined rulers, the first graders were asked to write about what they thought would happen. Then they performed the experiment and wrote about what they had learned. Sara's two-part entry, accompanied by a photocopied sheet describing the steps in the experiment and how to set it up, is one example of this category of message:

> I think the marbble that is on that rooler that is sidways is going to hit the other mabbles on the other rooler that isn't terned sidways and all the marbbles will fall off the rooler.
> We learned that the marbble that is on the rooler that is sidways pushes one that pushes another that pushes another that pushes the last one that rolls off the rooler and the one before the one that rolled off moved a little but it dasn't fall off.

Her father's reply indicated his interest and asked that Sara show the experiment to him at home. Having an interested audience for Family Message Journals encouraged in the students clear thinking to explore possible and actual outcomes, and coherent writing to explain that thinking and to accurately represent how experiments were carried out.

Writing to their families was also a way for the first graders to solve problems on paper and sometimes get families' helpful input. When Dina Carolan challenged her students to figure out how she could pick up a cup without touching it, they were invited to use their Family Message Journals to try to solve the problem. Kyle guessed at one possible solution:

> 3/18/97
> Dear famil
> can Mrs. carolan pick up a cup without tuching it she could ty

[tie] a Big not [knot] in The cup and put The not and put the
string Threw The Top and pull The string.

Kyle's mother replied that she thought Kyle's idea about attaching a
string to the cup with a knot might work, and other families suggested
trying the children's solutions at home to see how they worked. These
message exchanges demonstrate how the process of figuring out a
problem was not only supported by family members but sometimes
advanced by their feedback to messages.

The first graders also used their messages to figure out things by
questioning their families about specific situations or decisions which
puzzled them. Maryanne questioned why she was told she could not
pack her favorite beach towels for a trip to Florida. The opening
sentence of her message also exemplifies the children's sense that they
were conversing with families in their journals:

> April 15, 1997
> Dear Mommy I feel like talking abote Florida. When are we pack-
> ing up? I can't wait till tomorrow because Uncle and Aunt are
> comming from the PL. The beach will be fun but I hope there's no
> crabs! And a pool would be fun! But I still don't understand why
> evrybody can't take a beach towel. I disided that Im to worried to
> take my biny-babies not even one! I'll have to take some bord
> gams.
> > Love, Maryanne

In their reply, her family explained that beach towels would take up a lot
of space in their luggage and that they would be able to use the hotel's
towels while staying there. They also applauded her solution to the
problem of what to take to play with—board games were less likely to
get lost than the small stuffed toys called beanie babies.

Finally, the children sometimes used their messages to wonder on
paper and get families' input on a topic under exploration. Writing a
message about what she knew about owls after a series of lessons,
Kristen progressed to the topic of what owls eat and realized she was
not sure:

> owls protekt themselvs with ther wings ther beacs and ther feet.
> I think owls enamees are foxes hawcks and wolfs maibi [maybe]
> olws eat

In this message, Kristen took a shot at a new topic by generating ideas
about owls' possible enemies, but she really wasn't sure what owls
might eat. She left her message as is and waited to see if her family could
assist in this attempt to figure out the information she was wondering
about.

Developing and Appropriating a Functional Perspective on Writing

Chapter 4 explored the importance of writing for personal purposes on various topics and in varied formats. In this chapter, I have highlighted the importance of learning to write for various functions. The first graders were discovering the power of writing to get things done, influence others, share ideas and experiences, and get helpful input. Their discovery was directly linked to the learning of new genres. "Genres are functional . . . social actions," and their structures and strategies are central to communication, interaction, satisfying needs, and maintaining relationships (Cooper, 1999, p. 26).

It is important to note that the children were able to use their messages to achieve their own functions as well as those intended by their teachers. When their teachers invited them to write about plans for a school vacation, for example, many of the children used their messages to interact with their families or get something from them (e.g., requesting to be taken somewhere or to rent a video). Maryanne's message about Easter, which fell during the upcoming spring break, is a good example. Her lengthy message about all the Easter activities she enjoys began with a question:

> March 11, 1997
> Dear Mom and dad
> What do you want for easter. I cant wait till I find out what I get!
> And coloring the eggs and brining them to the chirch now that'll
> be fun won't it! oh gee! can I wait no! The easter bunny will be
> happy when he finds out that I left him a carrot and cabig and
> water and some picktures.
> Love, Maryanne

Maryanne began with a question to which she needed the answer in order to maintain her relationship with her family. She wanted to get her parents gifts they would like (with her older sister's help). The teacher did not foresee this interactional function, but Maryanne seized the opportunity to acquire information.

Other examples of children appropriating and capitalizing on the functional aspect of their Family Message Journal entries include integrating requests for a pet into a message assignment focused on sharing information about the animal and using a message about a special school event to express anger because a family member could not attend or had to leave early. In short, the children were not limited by the functions their teachers had in mind when they assigned message topics. Rather, the teachers' intentions were starting points, revealing to the students the many possibilities for Family Message Journal entries to help them accomplish their goals by enlisting their families' interest, appreciation, companionship, support, and resources. From these starting points, which broadened their repertoires of composition skills and strategies, the children often took off on their own.

A functional perspective on writing—with the focus on how writing affects an audience and moves the audience to action— complements the individual use of writing as a purposeful tool. This flip side of the power of writing is essential to carefully designed writing curricula. Because of its multifaceted nature and the centrality of writing for an audience, the Family Message Journal can play a prominent role in such curricula.

6 Families' Perspectives and Replies

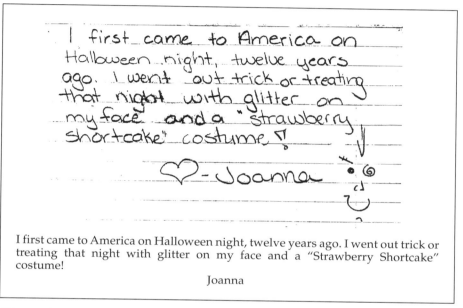

I first came to America on Halloween night, twelve years ago. I went out trick or treating that night with glitter on my face and a "Strawberry Shortcake" costume!

Joanna

Figure 6.1. Older siblings as well as adults sometimes participate in the Family Message Journal.

Unlike the other Family Message Journal entries which have introduced the chapters in this book, the message in Figure 6.1 was not written by a first grader but by her older sister. This is Joanna's reply to Maryanne's October message describing her Halloween plans. Halloween is a holiday with great significance for Joanna because she is a Polish immigrant who came to the United States with her family on Halloween night when *she* was in first grade. Therefore, it made sense that she was the family member who replied to Maryanne's message.

When a school contest to name the bulldog mascot was the topic of the first graders' messages, Maryanne used her entry to suggest the bulldog take the name of a popular musical group, the Bosstones. Again, it was fitting that her sister, a Bosstones fan, write the reply:

April 9
Hey Man, what's up? I think that Bosstones is an awesome name
for the Bulldog. I don't know if all of the kids in your class are
going to agree. But good luck anyway! Marcus thinks that
Bosstones is a really good name, too. Did I tell you that Bulldogs
are my friend Chantelle's favorite dog? Ask her sometime.
    Bye!
            Love, Joanna

In this chapter I look at Family Message Journals from the perspectives of the first graders' families. My focus here is not the families
themselves but rather what they wrote in their daily replies and their
views on the journals as a strategy for literacy instruction and family
involvement. Families may include parents, guardians, grandparents,
other relatives, siblings, and even close family friends. The four case-
study children I focus on in this book all lived with a mother, father, and
one or more siblings. Three of the first graders had older siblings to
whom messages were sometimes addressed, and like Joanna, two
occasionally replied in the Family Message Journals. The three students
with younger siblings also frequently included them as intended
recipients of their messages along with their parents.

As was typical of her peers, Kristen often worded her message
greeting "Dear Family" (or listed everyone's name) to be inclusive of all
family members. At times, however, she made a specific point of urging
that her sister, Melissa, read her messages:

6/10/97
Dear family,
I liked feild Day Because I came in second in the runing-rases
and I Liked tuger wor [tug-of-war] and when mr. bohan got hit
by a water Balloon I got a little wet at the Balloon toss so did
Jenny my partner we all had good sportmenship it was fun I came
in first plase in the sach-rase was hot and nise Love Kristen
ps. did you like it mom? 1. it was ok 2. I liked it or 3. I didn't like
it 1 2 3
I'll say I did like it I hope you did to I thot nuber [number] 2 did
you Beacuse I did aske dad if he liked it or melissa let her reed
my mesag I bet she wood of liked it.

Similarly, Sara tended to address her messages to "Mom, Dad,
and Rosa," but several entries, such as a Valentine poem, were about her
sister Rosa. Such messages included a written request that they be read
to her younger sibling.

Having siblings as well as adults involved in reading or listening
and responding to the children's messages not only expanded the
children's audience but also expanded the nature of family involve-

ment beyond its most common form, which includes only parents, often just the mother. As noted in Chapter 2, Family Message Journals were the only way for some of the children's fathers to participate in school activities because their work schedules tended to be less flexible than mothers'.

Sometimes both parents responded to the same message; multiple replies were found in three of the four case-study children's journals. In addition, Maryanne sometimes received replies from both a parent and her older sister. A winter message about polar bears prompted the following replies:

> Jan 14, 1997
> Dear Maryanne,
>   Brrr! Polar Bear makes me think of cold, snowy day! And I don't like cold, snowy days!
>   Brrr!
>   Love
>   Mommy

Joanna then added:

> You should fly south like a robin!

In cases like this, the Family Message Journal truly became a familywide tool for communication, as Joanna replied to her mother's message, which was a reply to Maryanne's original entry.

Parents' Perspectives

At the same time that teachers are being asked to increase parental involvement in children's education, parents report that they are experiencing increasing job-related demands on their time, making it difficult for them to become involved in their children's schooling on a daily basis, if at all. Nevertheless, after talking with parents of each of the case-study children, as well as informally chatting with many others, it became clear to me how committed parents and guardians were to making the Family Message Journal communication work, despite the constraints they experienced.

Dealing with Constraints

The most common and significant constraint parents discussed was time—they were on "tight schedules." Sometimes it was impossible to find time to read a child's message with him or her, write a reply, and then read it with the child after getting home late from work and before the child's bedtime. One solution was for a family member to write the reply after the first grader was asleep and then read it with the child the next morning during breakfast, or even while waiting at the school bus stop. Even if there was no time for this, replies were read again in school, so all children were able to enjoy their families' messages.

Some parents explained that scheduling a consistent time to read the messages and write a reply was helpful (for example, right after dinner). Some talked about the messages while dinner was heating in the microwave or during dinner. Some made the message exchange part of their bedtime routine, along with reading a story and brushing teeth.

Another strategy parents used to deal with the time constraint was to alternate replying so that neither mother nor father had to be responsible for it every night. And, of course, siblings also assisted at times. Though I did not interview the first graders' older siblings, parents said those siblings who took turns writing replies enjoyed participating, and their involvement was helpful when parents did not have time to reply. A few parents who said that occasionally they forgot to reply or did not have a chance explained that they always went back and "caught up" on their replies the next day.

Several parents told me they were initially concerned about what was expected of them as correspondents—they had feared they "would not do it right." These parents said it was helpful to receive, along with the children's first messages, the teachers' clear guidelines about what was expected in replies and a reminder of the purpose of the journal communication. Parents were also reassured by the teachers' willingness to talk with them about any concerns or uncertainties that arose and to explain things like "letter format" without making parents feel ignorant. In fact, many said that it was actually quite easy and took very little time to reply once they understood what was expected of them and did not have to spend time worrying about what or how to write. Most of the parents described Family Message Journals as "easy" and "workable" once they got used to them. One or two, however, resented that teachers expected them to spend any time on school-related work—they saw this as solely the teacher's role. The case-study families did not share this belief, but there is a good possibility that a couple of families in any classroom will.

Recognizing the Value of Family Message Journals

Despite the challenges they sometimes faced in keeping up their end of the correspondence, parents were nearly unanimous in the opinion that Family Message Journals were "a great strategy" or "a really good idea." They described a number of benefits. First, the journals forced families to spend time together reading and talking about each others' messages. Several parents said they valued this "contact" or "additional time spent together." In a busy day, it is easy for working parents *not* to find extra time for their children—the Family Message Journals made them "find time to do it."

Parents also valued the way in which the journals involved the whole family in their children's education, "not just the mothers, who were more likely to be involved anyway." Some parents recognized that this strategy opened up family involvement to all parents, including those whose work or home schedules are not flexible enough to allow them ever to visit school and who therefore are usually excluded from family involvement initiatives. One parent described it as "a subtle way to really involve families," letting them know how much their participation is needed and valued, and relying on them to do their part without asking them to change their daily schedules.

Parents commented appreciatively on how the journals gave them an authentic role in expanding or extending children's school learning—"I could add what I know about what they wrote about" or "connect school lessons to experiences we've had as a family, like our trip to Plymouth."

Another aspect of Family Message Journals which many discussed was that they kept parents informed. As one parent commented, "It helped me really know what they were doing in school." Parents also liked the way in which the journals sparked school-related discussions at home—"I knew what was happening in the classroom and we could talk about it at home." In addition, some parents were pleased to see that the message writing in school encouraged self-initiated writing at home. Children got in the habit of writing letters to relatives, or stories or poems as a leisure time activity; they had discovered the many uses of writing in their lives. Parents felt strongly that this discovery was an outgrowth of the Family Message Journals because they noted many similarities in form and content between the children's messages and their self-initiated writing.

Mothers and fathers also commented on how Family Message Journals documented children's progress in writing, reading, and subject-area learning. Some explained that at first they were "worried about my kid's writing." But with the teachers' help in understanding that the invented spellings and occasional letter reversals were normal developmental markers, these worried parents were able to recognize the strengths in their children's writing rather than focus on the errors. Being able to look at their children's work collected in the journal notebook over the course of several months provided parents with ample evidence of their children's progress in all aspects of writing. I discuss this progress further in the next chapter.

Perhaps the most convincing evidence of how much parents valued the Family Message Journals is the fact that twenty out of twenty-four families wrote replies to their children *every* night. Others wrote back at least a couple of times a week, and, as mentioned previously, occasionally a family replied to a message a day late. Only one family did not write back. (As noted in Chapter 3, the teachers rounded up other correspondents for children as needed, including student teachers; older "buddy" students in the building; the principal; Title I, resource, and special teachers; and senior or parent volunteers in the school.) While this high rate of participation might not be found in all schools, it is typical of the family response Dina Carolan and Karen Wilensky experience every year in their classrooms.

Their success in enlisting family participation is due in part to the fact that these teachers make it clear that they take the children's writing seriously as a form of communication with families. This is evident in the kinds of messages they assign. For example, they give the first graders responsibility for telling their families when there will be a change in their daily school routine, or what they need to bring to school for a field trip or other special event. Having children use the Family Message Journal to share important information suggests to parents that the children's writing warrants attention. In addition, Karen has found that a telephone call to parents reminding them of how important their participation is often helps get straggling participants fully and regularly involved in the Family Message Journal communication. It is also worth noting that Family Message Journals are only one aspect of a first-grade classroom culture and structure, described in Chapter 3, that reflects Dina's and Karen's commitment to working with families as partners. They clearly expect families to be involved in children's learning in many ways.

Dina's and Karen's success with Family Message Journals suggests there is little ground for the defeatist attitude that parents just don't care and won't take the time to participate in such an activity. Realistically, parents told me, it is not always easy to find even fifteen minutes to sit with a child, read his or her message, write a reply, and have the child read it. But despite the constraints parents identified, they made the strategy work because they believed it was worth it. Their comments on the various benefits of Family Message Journals help explain why participation was so widespread.

Families' Replies

As I did with the children's messages, through constant comparative analysis of all of the families' replies I searched for emergent patterns leading to a category system for describing the communicative functions of the replies (Glaser & Strauss, 1967). The resulting categories illuminate the nature of families' replies and suggest how they might contribute to children's content-area and literacy learning. Families' replies fell into seven general categories. The replies served to:

1. demonstrate interest in children's ideas and learning and ask children to tell more
2. expand children's knowledge by providing new information
3. share personal opinions and stories
4. acknowledge good ideas and vow to try them
5. ask questions to encourage thinking and problem solving
6. suggest solutions to problems
7. model a range of writing options

Demonstrating Interest

Many of the families' replies to the first graders' messages demonstrated interest in their children's ideas and information. Chapter 5 discussed how some of these replies reinforced children's sense of having expertise to share. But these replies not only empowered children as information-givers, they were also motivating—they indicated that family members truly enjoyed reading the first graders' messages, and this inspired the young writers.

Kyle wrote about an experiment with soft- and hard-boiled eggs:

> 3/27/97
> Dear Mom did you know how to tell the difrins uv a hard boled [boiled] spinslike a top the soft boled egg dosiant spin love kyle

His mother replied:

> Dear Kyle
> No, I didn't know that. Thanks for the information.
> Love
> Mom

Her "thanks for the information" showed Kyle that she was interested in what he had discovered.

Similarly, Maryanne's mother showed interest in the information Maryanne had shared about how bears can grow ten feet tall:

October 20th, 1996
DEAR (BEAR) MARYANNE!
    NO, I DID NOT KNOW THAT BEARS CAN BE <u>THAT</u> TALL!
I REALLY DON'T WANT TO MEET A HUNGRY, 10 FEET TALL
BEAR. O NO!
                        LOVE
                            Mommy

Many of her mother's replies demonstrated this kind of enthusiastic engagement with the information Maryanne had included in her message. Another one read:

Jan. 29, 1997
Dear Maryanne,
    I have learned something new from you today.
    That groundhog and woodchuck are two different names for
    the same animal!
    And I know very well what this cute animal likes to eat!
    <u>Our</u> tomatos! Do you remember "our woodchuck"?
        Love
                Mommy

Her mother was particularly interested in Maryanne's message because it related to a family gardening experience.

It was common for families' messages to express genuine excitement about children's learning and even pride in how much their youngsters knew. Again, a typical example comes from Maryanne's journal:

March 5, 1997
Dear Maryanne,
    And again I learned a new thing from you.
    I never knew that calico cats are all girls!
    Isn't school great?
You learn something new every day. And I learn from you! For sure,
sometimes I know things you are just learning, but that is o.k.
        Love
                Mommy

Maryanne's mother admits that she already knows some of the information her daughter is learning but confirms that much of the information Maryanne includes in her messages is enlightening.

In another reply, Maryanne's mother demonstrated her interest in a message by giving specific feedback on what she noticed and enjoyed about the story of the kite who was afraid of heights:

March 19, 1997
    I like your story very much. I would never think to make a
kite afraid of heights in <u>my</u> story.

So good that the boy who bought the kite, pulled it back down, when he felt the wind getting strong.

It was a very safe thing to do!

I hope that the kite and the boy became good friends and spent a lot of time together, having a good time!
                    Love
                        Mommy

Sometimes replies demonstrated families' interest by asking children to tell more about the topic of their messages. Another message consisting of the beginning of a story prompted the following reply:

March 6, 1997
Dear Maryanne,
    The story you have started to write sounds very interesting.
    I wonder if the dog will be friendly or not. And I wonder how Pickles looks!
    I hope Pickles and the dog become friends.
    I can't wait to read the story when you finish it.
            Love
                Mommy

Not only did this reply demonstrate interest in what Maryanne had written, but the questions her mother asked encouraged completion of the story.

Other replies also asked children to tell more—to elaborate on their ideas or information. When Kristen wrote that "next's week's show-and-tell is my choice. I want to bring," followed by a drawing of a teddy bear, her mother replied:

Dear Kristen,
    What bear are you going to bring?
            Love,
                Mom

Sara's mother also asked for more information when Sara wrote:

4/14/97
Dear Family
We are having a game today and it's caled spelling baseball. you can spell single dubl and tripls and homeruns Love Sara

Her mother was clearly interested and questioned:

Dear Sara,
    I would like to know more about spelling baseball. Are homerun words very hard to spell? What is it like playing spelling baseball?
    Pretty soon you'll be playing real baseball. I think it will be fun.
        Love, Mommy

Not only did such messages indicate interest in learning more, but they also suggested ways in which the first graders might elaborate in their future writing to satisfy their readers' curiosity.

Providing New Information

Just like talented teachers, families noticed many opportunities to use their replies to capitalize on "teachable moments," when children were receptive to learning because of their involvement in the topic of the message exchange. Often families' replies expanded children's knowledge by providing new, related information.

The first graders were involved in a schoolwide fund-raiser, and their teachers asked them to inform their families about this project in a message:

> September 13, 1996
> Oh Boy! I hoPe I caN sell some gifts! Yes No
> LOVE, MARYANNE

Maryanne's father replied:

> September 15 96'
> DEAR MARYANNE!
> WE HOPE YOU WILL BE A GOOD "SALESMAN" — "SALES-
> GIRL" AND YOU WILL "EMPLOY" MOM AND ME TO HELP
> YOU.
>   LOVE DAD

Typical of many families' replies throughout the year, Maryanne's father's message introduced new vocabulary, in this case related to sales work, the topic of her message.

When Maryanne wrote a message about pine needles and how they "are covered with wax and stay green in the winter," her mother and father paired up to write a message in which they introduced the term *evergreen* and the names of other types of evergreen trees:

> Dec. 4, 1996
> Hi Maryanne!
> The pine tree   PINE
> The spruce tree   SPRUCE
> The fir tree   FIR
> The hemlock tree   HEMLOCK
> All these trees have needles and are green all year round.
>   So we call them EVERGREENS.
>   LOVE
>   Dad and Mom

Sometimes the information families shared with their children was even more substantive than the introduction of new vocabulary. A Thanksgiving message in the form of a riddle prompted the following reply:

> Nov. 19, 1996
> Dear Maryanne,
> The answer to your riddle is: PILGRIMS.
> Do you know, that in our times people, who leave their country and go to another country to make their home there are called "IMMIGRANTS"?
>
> And you are a daughter of Polish immigrants!
> > Love
> > > Your Mama

Another reply provided information related to Maryanne's message explaining that "Washington Street [the local main street] was named after George Washington!"

> Feb. 11, 1997
> Dear Maryanne,
> To give a person's name to a place, a street, or a building is very popular in the world.
> Most often these people did something very important and GOOD for their country or for all the people in the world (like finding a medicine for some illnesses).
> > Love
> > > Mommy

Maryanne's mother used the specific instance her daughter had learned about to teach more general sociohistorical knowledge.

Sara's father likewise shared new information in response to a message that was part of a unit of study on wind:

> 3/11/97
> Dear Sara,
> You told me about lots of good things the wind does when it blows gently.
> Sometimes the wind blows very very hard and is a hurricane or a tornado. A hurricane can blow sailboats out of the water and onto the land. A tornado is so strong that it could lift up our whole house! I'm glad there aren't tornados in [our town]!
> > Love, Papa

This reply broadened Sara's knowledge by telling the "other side of the story."

Sara's mother also tried to broaden her child's understanding. Sara had written a message about trees, focusing on carbon dioxide and oxygen production and consumption. Her mother replied:

> Dear Sara,
>   We help trees by giving them carbon dioxide and they help us by giving us some of the oxygen we need to breathe. But trees also help us in other ways. They make our world beautiful and they give us wood to make things. How can we help trees and show them we appreciate what they do for us? I think we are lucky to have a yard <u>full</u> of trees, especially the dogwood.
>   Love,
>   Mommy

This reply offers another way of thinking about people's interdependence with trees and our responsibility to care for nature.

A message written by Maryanne about the coming of spring prompted a reply in which her father tried to raise her awareness of the many changes she could observe around her as one season gradually replaced another:

> Dear Maryanne!
> Spring is comming
>
> You can tell
>
> A week ago the lake was covered with ice.
> lat sunday we saw just very little ice on southern edge of the lake.
>
> Spring is comming. . .
>
> We will see how much our lake changes durring this week. . .
>
> So guess what . . . where are we going to go this comming sunday?
>   Your Daddy

Finally, some replies provided the first graders with specific information about writing well. These replies were responses to messages consisting of stories composed by the students or story webs created after reading a book. Sara's mother wrote about using a story web as a prewriting planner:

> Dear Sara,
>   I really think your Story Web is wonderful! It shows how well you understood the story. Making a web like this can also help you when you are planning to write a story. I love the stories you write!
>   Love,
>   Mommy

Maryanne's mother introduced other writing strategies when Maryanne began a story about Florida, where she had vacationed:

May 8, 1997
Dear Maryanne,
   I like the beginning of your story. I hope you will put some interesting characters in your story. Maybe you could use some of your experiences from vacations? Maybe some animals you saw or plants that grow there? Try it!
      I can't wait to read it when you are done!
                           Love
                              Mommy

This reply taught Maryanne techniques she could use in any writing: including interesting characters, drawing on her own life experiences, and adding realistic details, such as animals and plants that fit the setting of her story. Replies suggesting such techniques are yet another example of how adept families can be at providing beneficial instruction when given the opportunity to get this involved.

Sharing Personal Opinions and Stories

Sometimes the first graders' messages shared their opinions and family members replied by offering theirs. When Kristen wrote about why she likes pie, her father shared his thoughts:

11/15/96
Dear Kristen,
   I love when you and Mommy make apple pies. I love the smell.
   Love
   Dad

On the first day back at school after New Year's Day, children were asked to write a wish for the world. Sara wrote:

1/3/97
Dear mom dad and Rosa
MY wiSh for the world in 1997 is thet ol [all] the dogS and catS hav a hoam Love sara

Her mother and father each wrote a reply:

Dear Sara,
   What a wonderful wish you made! I wish that all the people have homes and enough healthy food. I hope our wishes come true.
   Love, Mommy

1/5/97
Dear Sara,
I wish all of the people fighting wars all around the world could make peace with one another.
   Love, Papa

This type of exchange of opinion opened up new perspectives for the children; they were able to see what others believed or wished for and could then talk with their families about why.

The first graders' messages also frequently elicited related stories of family members' experiences. Maryanne wrote:

> October 11 1996
> AW Mom + DAd, Alex mai feel sad. HeS peT DiD Love
> MARYANNE

In reply, her mother sympathized, telling her own story of loss:

> October 15, 1996
> Hi Maryanne!
>   I am sure Alex <u>is</u> sad. I was <u>very</u> sad when my pet died. I cried
> a lot!
>   Love
>   Mommy

Families shared happier stories as well. Maryanne wrote a message about mittens in response to a book she had read. Her mother replied with a drawing of mittens and a personal story that recaptured her childhood feelings:

> January 23, 1997
> Dear Maryanne,
>   Mittens are great! I loved mittens when I was a little girl. I
> had a pair of the best mittens in the whole world— they were
> made of lamb skin with the fur inside of them. So soft and warm!
> I used them also as pockets and kept things in them. I hope you
> will have a great pair of mittens too!
>   Love Mommy

Maryanne's message about silent "e," the "magic" letter that can "turn a cap into a cape," prompted the following reply:

> December 18 96
> Dear Maryanne
>   BEFORE WE CAME TO THIS COUNTRY, WE HAD NO IDEA
> THAT SILENT "E" EXISTS . . .
>   IT WAS FUNNY HOW WE HAD PRONOUNCE SOME
> WORDS WITH LOUD "E" INSTEAD KEEPING IT SILENT . . .
> IT WAS FUNNNN TO LEARN ALL THIS "MAGIC TRICKS"
> AND WE ARE STILL LEARNING
>   DADDY

Maryanne's father told the story of learning English as a second language and the mistakes he and her mother made at first.

Another message, about sorting buttons, led him to tell an older family story:

October 17th 96
DEAR MARYANNE!
I WOULD LIKE YOU TO KNOW THAT YOUR GREAT, GREAT
MA <u>LOVED </u>BUTTONS! SHE LOVED JEWEL BUTTONS THE
MOST . . .
BUT SHE LOVED "BUTTONS BUTTONS" TOO . . .
SHE HAD A HUGE BUTTON COLLECTION.
   I LIKE THEM TOO
       LOVE DADDY "BUTTON"

Her father's reply introduced Maryanne to her great grandmother's hobby. In this way, Family Message Journals can extend beyond the immediate family and keep family lore alive.

Acknowledging Good Ideas

Families' replies sometimes acknowledged the first graders' good ideas and even vowed to try them, if appropriate. When Sara wrote a preelection day message about what she would do if she were president ("giv the por people munee"), her mother affirmed that she had a good idea:

11/4/96
Dear Sara,
    If you were running for President I would vote for you. I'm
glad you care about poor people and want to help others.
       Love, Mommy

Maryanne's message asking for a diary also received a reply acknowledging the good idea:

April 13, 1997
Dear Maryanne,
    My answer is <u>Yes</u>. Yes, you will get the book you would like
to have.
I think, that writing notes every day or so is good for you for many reasons.
First: you practice writing,
Second: you never forget when things happen,
Third: it is so much fun to read about yourself when you grow up
. . .
       Love Mommy

This reply not only told Maryanne *why* keeping a diary is a good idea but also included a promise that her mother would follow through on the idea by purchasing one.

Maryanne's September message asking for a "noo dogee" also was successful—her father acknowledged that it was a good idea and vowed to try to get a dog soon:

> Dear Maryanne!
> We all would like to have a dog . . .
> And we will try to get it next year . . .
>   Mommy and I hope that all of our house projects will be done
> so there will be time enough to care for a dog.
> P.S. By the way I liked the "open house" at your school very much.
>   Love Dad

Her family *did* like the idea—Maryanne had a new dog by the end of the school year.

Sara also wrote a message asking for a pet. Her father, too, valued the idea and suggested a way to explore the possibility:

> Dear Sara,
> Maybe we can look at some books to learn more about what it's
> like to take care of a turtle at home.
>   Love, Papa

Finally, Maryanne's message sharing her knowledge of Abraham Lincoln's life story made her mother think of an idea she wanted to try:

> Feb. 6, 1997
> Dear Maryanne,
>   I am really impressed! You wrote so much about Abraham
> Lincoln! And I learned something new again!
>   I think we should start writing stories from our families his-
> tory. Some day it will be interesting to read!
>   Love
>   Mommy

At the same time she acknowledged that her daughter's message had given her a good idea, Maryanne's mother also affirmed the power of writing to preserve memories.

Asking Questions

Family Message Journal replies often consisted of or included questions which encouraged the first graders to think and solve problems. When Kristen wrote about being able to make an "L" with her left hand, her mother responded:

> 12/10/96
> Dear Kristen,
>   What other letters can you make with your left and right
> hands?
>   What hand do you write with? I write with my right hand.
> Love, Mom

This reply encouraged Kristen to explore letter forms she could create using her hands.

A message about how seeds fall out of dried pine cones and scatter led to questions in many Family Message Journal replies. Sara's father's reply was typical:

> 12/4/96
> Dear Sara,
> What happens to the seeds after they scatter on the ground?
> Love, Papa

This question and others like it asked children to think more about the topic and try out possible ideas. It also suggested something about writing well: readers often have questions when the information provided is not complete; writers need to elaborate on their topics to satisfy their audience.

Other family replies included questions which aroused children's curiosity and sometimes got them involved in further research at school, at home, or in the town library with family members:

> 10/7/96
> Dear Sara,
> Did Johnny Appleseed plant any other kinds of trees besides apple trees?
>
> Love, Papa

Or:

> 1/14/97
> Dear Sara,
>   Cardinals are very pretty birds. How do you think they keep warm in the winter? Some kinds of birds fly south to where it is warmer, but not Cardinals.
>   Love,
>   Mommy

These relatively simple, brief replies from early in the year nevertheless contained thought-provoking questions that were followed up through family discussion and research.

An example of a more complex question that aroused awareness and curiosity comes from Maryanne's Family Message Journal later in the year:

> Dear Maryanne,
>   Your list of things that a seed needs is very precise.
>   I hope that our potato plant will grow very nicely, beacuse we have given it every thing from your list . . .
>   But I wonder how it happens that some plants grow with very little of soil, water or space. Like in a little crack in the rock or between bricks or in the smallest crack in the pavement? How is it possible?
>   Love Mommy

When Maryanne wrote that animals should not be kept in cages, even though in some cases zoo cages protect endangered animals from extinction, her father replied:

> March 30, 1997
> Dear Maryanne!
> LETS TALK ABOUT ANIMALS THAT ARE BETTER OFF AS PETS
> HOW MANY CAN YOU NAME:
>
> CIVILISATION HURTS BUT IT ALSO HELPS
> WE HUMANS ARE PART OF NATURE
> AND WE SHOULD NOT ALLOWE TO HURT THE NATURE
>   DADDY

In the space her father left, Maryanne answered his question, listing seven animals that make good pets ("dogs, cats, white mice, hampsters, ginny pigs, goldfish, cannarrie"). This reply encouraged her to think not only of pet animals but also about the advantages of keeping animals as pets, though they may be caged, and about human beings' responsibility toward animals.

In another reply, Maryanne's father shared his knowledge of bats and related folklore, and posed a question for his daughter to consider:

> 3/10/97
> Dear Maryanne!
>   Bats are very nice creatures, although some of us do not like them . . .
> . . . Probably because of some legends.
> I like them beacuse they are smart.
>   I like them because they are good to keep the ballance in our environment.
>   I like them beacuse they catch mosquitoes and some other pesti flies.
> There are quite a few in the woods in our backyard.
> Do you like them or are you affraid of them?
>   Love
>   Daddy

This seemingly simple question is made more complex for Maryanne by her father's enumeration of bats' positive qualities, despite their reputation as frightening. She considered his message and replied: "I like them."

Another reply from Maryanne's father/tooth fairy included a variety of questions related to Maryanne's message about the tooth fairy:

JANUARY 6 1997
DEAR MARYANNE
DO YOU KNOW, HOW MANY OF YOUR TEETH I HAD
FOUND UNDER YOU PILLOW
DO YOU REMEMBER?
I DO . . .
DID YOU THINK WHICH ONE WILL BE NEXT FOR YOU
TO LOOSE AND ME TO FIND?
HOW MANY TEETH DO YOU HAVE NOW?
DO YOU KNOW HOW MANY WILL YOU HAVE WHEN
YOU WILL BE AS OLD AS JOANNA?
PLEASE WRITE TO ME ABOUT IT
YOUR TOOTH FAIRY

Some of these questions Maryanne could answer by asking family members, others she could figure out on her own (e.g., by counting her own teeth), and some required further reading or other research about dental development.

Some questions in families' replies challenged children to solve a problem or come up with an idea on their own—there were no fact-based answers to these. Sara's mother asked such a question in her reply to Sara's message about the Thanksgiving story:

11/26/96
Dear Sara,
I'm glad the Native Americans helped the Pilgrims or the Pilgrims might have starved. What could the Pilgrims do to thank the Native Americans for their help?
Love,
Mommy

A similar thought-provoking question was posed by Maryanne's father when replying to a message about the first graders' study of snowflakes:

January 21 '97
DEAR MARYANNE!
SNOW FLAKES ARE
LIKE
PEOPLE
There are NOT TWO ALIKE
Is it good or bad
Think about it and tell me tomorrow.
P.S. Snowflakes have six sides
How many "sides" do we have?
- good
- bad
- ....
- ....
Your Daddy

And, finally, some questions were playful rather than serious, as in the reply to Maryanne's message about pajama day at school:

> March 23, 1997
> Dear Maryanne,
>   Daddy had an idea about a pajama party at our house. I don't think it is a good idea beacuse our friends may feel embarrassed to show up in their nightgowns or pajamas. Maybe we should just have a regular party? What do you think? Yes No
>   Love Mommy

Maryanne's answer was "no," do not have a regular party; have an adult pajama party!

Suggesting Solutions

Occasionally the first graders wrote about problems or concerns in their Family Message Journals, and in reply families tried to allay the children's worries or help them cope with or solve their problems. For example, Maryanne, a creative, talented artist who loved to draw animals, was uneasy about having her work selected for display in the townwide student art show. She expressed her concerns in a message inviting families to the show. Her mother replied:

> Dear Maryanne,
>   You worry too much about the art show, because you do not remember that the art show is simply a presentation of drawing, sculptures, and other pieces of art done by students of all schools in [town]. You liked it, when your big sister was there. Remember?
>   For sure you liked all the pictures of animals there.
>   Love, mommy

Whereas Maryanne's mother tried to reassure her daughter, her father, replying to a message of disappointment at losing a game, advised Maryanne to take a realistic perspective:

> January 22 '97
> DEAR MARYANNE!
> GAMES ARE, AND ALWAYS HAD BEEN ABOUT WINNING OR LOSING
> Sometimes TIE . . .
> LIFE IS VERY ALIKE
> SO: BE HAPPY WHEN YOU WIN
>   DO NOT CRY WHEN YOU LOSE
>   AND TRY TO LEARN WHEN YOU TIE
>   Winn Loose Tie DADDY

Her father suggested to Maryanne a way of dealing with and thinking philosophically about the outcome of a game.

Sara's message of anger at a friend's behavior elicited the following reply:

12/9/96
Dear Sara,
Sometimes people do things that make us feel mad or sad without meaning to hurt our feelings. When this happens, try telling the other person how you feel. Maybe they will say they are sorry.
Love, Papa

This reply suggested action Sara could take to feel better.

Maryanne's mother also suggested a solution to the problem of a friend's annoying bragging:

04-10-97
Dear Maryanne,
Many, many people, even grownups like to brag about things. Most often to feel good about their . . . (whatever it is they brag about), and to get ATTENTION. And you know yourself how important it is to get it!
So, when your friends do brag, give them what they need, and go ahead and play!
Love Mommy

Modeling Writing Options

Families' replies not only taught the children new information and suggested ways of elaborating on their ideas, thinking about issues, and coping with problems, but they also modeled a range of writing styles, techniques, and conventions. This range expanded the first graders' awareness of how writing can function and what forms it can take. As the examples throughout this chapter show, replies modeled letter format, various greetings and closings, ways of dating a message, punctuation conventions, postscripts, and many genres, styles, and stances toward one's reader. These daily models from home complemented and reinforced the instruction and modeling of techniques and conventions that the first-grade teachers provided in the classroom.

Modeling Genre and Form

Experimentation with genre and form was common in the families' replies, demonstrating that there are various ways of approaching any topic. Sometimes the families wrote stories like the mitten memory shared by Maryanne's mother; sometimes they described something or presented information in narrative form, like Sara's mother in her entry about how we benefit from trees. Other replies presented facts in list form, like the evergreen list by Maryanne's father or her mother's list of reasons why it is good to keep a diary. Many replies, by Maryanne's father in particular, were written in poetic form. Some replies demonstrated common expository essay structures, like the entry comparing and contrasting snowflakes and people, and the one presenting two sides on the issue of bats.

Modeling Qualities of Good Writing

Families' replies also demonstrated qualities of good writing that can be found in *any* genre. For example, replying to Maryanne's message about taking a walk to look for cardinals, her mother wrote:

> January 14, 1997
> Dear Maryanne,
> I liked our walk across the snowy playground on Sunday. It was a very beautiful day!
> Blue sky, sun, and snow covered with diamonds.
> And our snow angels came out so good!
> I had a great time!
> Love
> Mommy

This reply includes a metaphor to capture the visual experience of the walk, helping any reader picture and appreciate the scene.

Another quality of good writing is focus. Families' replies modeled how to stay focused on a topic even when looking at its various aspects. Maryanne's mother accomplished this in her reply about the walk, setting the scene by recalling where they walked, describing the experience visually, commenting on the activity of making snow angels, and closing with a general statement of her feelings about the outing. Other replies modeling focus and elaboration include the one Maryanne's mother wrote about the custom of naming streets after famous people and Sara's father's entry on various wind storms and their impact. These replies showed the first graders how to include enough information or elaborate enough on one's ideas to satisfy readers' curiosity or needs.

Another way in which families' replies modeled elaboration was to demonstrate how to connect new information to their daily lives. An example is the reply by Maryanne's mother about woodchucks and groundhogs in which she makes the connection to seeing these animals eat from the family garden. The entry written by Sara's mother about trees likewise relates relatively abstract information to the dogwood tree in Sara's front yard. Good writing manages to make the abstract concrete or personally meaningful, or to create a sense of immediacy about seemingly distant information or situations. Families' replies often modeled how to do this.

Modeling Language

The language of some replies was informal and conversational, as in "You worry too much about the art show." Other replies seemed more formal and carefully structured, such as "Your list of things that a seed needs is very precise." Families' shifting language use modeled what was appropriate for different types of replies. The first of these two message exchanges was a more personal, emotional one; the second was focused on objective fact. Some replies were serious in nature and tone, like the one Sara's father wrote suggesting letting others know if they hurt your feelings. His serious tone fit the serious topic of the message. However, playful language, jokes, and riddles were also common in the Family Message Journals. Sara's father wrote another reply (to a message about owls) in the form of a riddle:

> 3/6/97
> Dear Sara,
> Knock knock
> Who's there?
> Hoo
> Hoo who?
> Are you an owl too?
> Love, Papa

And when he replied to a message about spiders, Sara's father included a joke along with some new information:

> 4/29/97
> Dear Sara,
> Did you know that spiders have 8 eyes around the top of their heads? It's very hard to sneak up on a spider!
> Love, Papa

Jokes and riddles were also common in Kyle's Family Message Journal. In response to a message about growing mold and looking at it under a microscope, Kyle's father joked about the condition of his son's bedroom:

Dear Kyle,
    I think that mold escaped from your room! Please don't bring
it back home, or else! Your Dad

Kyle's mother, like Sara's father, shared an owl riddle as one of her replies:

Dear Kyle,
What did the owl say when someone came to his door?
Who who who?
                    Love
                    Mom

When Kyle wrote that he could make a capital L with his left hand, his mother replied:

Dear Kyle,
Dad has the flu with a capital F. I liked your crazy writing.
    Au revoir,
            Mom
    Je t'aime!
    mon petit chou

This playful reply also taught a figure of speech *and* incorporated a second language. Some families regularly included such second language greetings, closings, and brief messages, modeling how to code-switch within a written message, as they did at home orally at times.

Though not every family modeled a full range of options for message writing, as a group the first graders were introduced to a wide range of models when children shared their families' replies in the classroom. Their teachers sometimes took this opportunity to highlight certain aspects of the replies, making children more aware of the qualities of strong writing and the many options open to writers.

Modeling the Unconventional

Families' replies were not always fully conventional, in part because some were still learning Standard English, but this did not seem to affect the children's development as conventional writers (discussed in Chapter 7). They were exposed to plenty of conventional grammar, spelling, punctuation, and text formats in their other reading and writing in the classroom and at home (reading at home was assigned as nightly homework). Further, some of the families' unconventional composition styles were not unlike the experimentation with form that marks the work of acclaimed novelists, poets, and essayists. Regardless of which conventions families overlooked or experimented with, the children were all receiving the powerful message that writing communicates and maintains relationships.

Scaffolding Children's Learning

Just as caregivers adjust their conversational roles when children are first learning to talk (Cazden, 1988; Ninio & Bruner, 1978; Ratner & Bruner, 1978), the first graders' families were sensitive to the need to scaffold the written exchange of ideas. Though they may not have been consciously aware they were doing so, families usually composed replies that were manageable for young children who were emergent to beginning readers and writers. And throughout the year, they gauged their replies to match the children's growing competencies. Readers who have been paying attention to the dates on replies may have already noticed this gradual transition.

Replies changed significantly over the course of the year. In all of the Family Message Journals, early replies tended to be brief and to consist of simple sentences in narrative form. They were written in neat print, sometimes all capital letters, which are often taught before lowercase letters to children at home, in preschool, and in kindergarten. Occasionally parents rewrote replies when they realized they had forgotten to print or write neatly enough for their replies to be legible for the first graders. Over time, replies grew longer, sentences more complex, and handwriting less painstaking, and new genres and formats were included.

The content of families' replies changed over time as well, also becoming more complex. Early replies focused on introducing new vocabulary and on shared experiences, but later replies included more difficult, complex concepts like the pros and cons of an issue, considering different perspectives, and more abstract information unrelated to shared experiences. As the year progressed, children were also asked more challenging questions. For example, an early question to Sara was: "Did Johnny Appleseed plant any other kinds of trees besides apple trees?" This was the full reply her father wrote. But later in the year Sara was asked more open-ended questions, such as: "How can we help trees and show them we appreciate what they do for us?" This two-part question was embedded in a much longer reply. Like the best teachers, families were responsive to children's needs and seemed to know how to "read" the children's messages to interpret what they were ready for in a reply. Families met the children where they were in the learning process, adjusting their replies to continually challenge the first graders as readers and thinkers without frustrating them.

7 Family Message Journals Document Growth

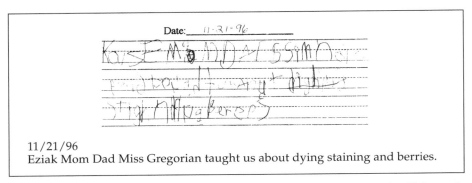

11/21/96
Eziak Mom Dad Miss Gregorian taught us about dying staining and berries.

Figure 7.1. The nearly illegible print in this journal entry written by Kyle early in the school year is characteristic of some emergent writers' messages.

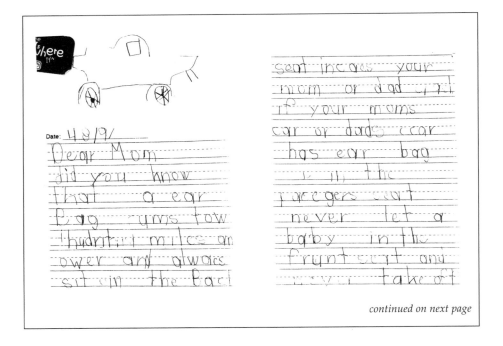

continued on next page

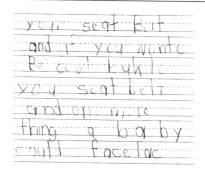

4/8/97
Did you know that an air bag comes two hundred miles an hour? And always sit in the back seat in case your mom or dad crashes. If your mom or your dad's car has air bags in the passenger seat never let a baby in the front seat and never take off your seat belt. And if you want to be cool buckle you seat belt. And one more thing, a baby should face back.

Figure 7.2. Kyle's "air bag" message, written four and a half months later, shows considerable progress in writing development.

Kyle's message in Figure 7.1, regarding a school visitor who taught the first graders about dying and weaving wool to make rugs, is nearly illegible. The mixed lowercase and capital letters in each of the first six words were written in reverse order, and each letter itself is written in reverse orientation. For example, "taught" was spelled "thguat," with each of the letters within the word reversed as well. There is no space between words. The handwriting in the message in Figure 7.2, written four and a half months later, reflects considerable growth—individual letters are well formed with few reversals, capitalization conventions are generally observed, left-to-right order is followed within words, and spacing is used to separate words.

Though the surface-level changes in handwriting from the November to the April messages are the most immediately noticeable, there are other areas of enormous growth as well. The content of Kyle's second message demonstrates greater audience awareness and a growing ability to express his ideas in writing. This message opens with an attention-getting question and is much longer and more complete than the first. He tells everything he remembers about the lesson on automobile safety, showing how much he has learned on the topic. Moreover, he explains *why* it is important to follow safety rules: in case there is a crash; because airbags inflate with great force. Readers sense the conviction behind his message—his voice comes through. In addition, the format of this message more closely matches letter format, with a date, a greeting, and the beginning of the message on the next line. Finally, Kyle has moved from relying on phonetic spelling and copying words to a greater reliance on sight words and transitional spellings, such as using the familiar, correctly spelled "ear" for "air," and spelling "bukle" by using the "-le" spelling pattern he has learned for the "l" sound at the end of a word.

Like Kyle's examples, every child's Family Message Journal entries are a window on his or her evolving abilities as a writer. Because the journals are a daily activity, they result in a large body of work, providing ample evidence of students' growth over time. Since all entries are in essentially the same format, those from weeks or months apart can be compared to determine children's specific areas of strength, signs of development, and areas needing improvement. Because there are so many entries, teachers have solid ground upon which to make such judgments. Although I found that the quality of individual entries varied with the first graders' interest in the topic, the length of time they had to write, and the individual child's mood, as a group the entries from each student's journal gave a clear, consistent picture of where each one stood in his or her writing development at any point in time.

In this chapter, I focus on how teachers can use Family Message Journals systematically, as naturalistic evidence to evaluate children's literacy development and learning across the curriculum. I also discuss how families can be involved in the evaluation process and how children, too, can participate in self-assessment of their journals. Although the primary purpose of Family Message Journals is literacy learning and family involvement, the journals demonstrate how evaluation can complement rather than detract from these goals.

Teacher Evaluation

Though children's Family Message Journals completely filled large-capacity three-ring binders by the end of the school year, first-grade teacher Dina Carolan developed a manageable way of looking at children's journal entries across time. To avoid being overwhelmed by the sheer volume, she selected one entry from September and then two or three entries each month thereafter to place in each child's portfolio notebook. This portfolio notebook was divided into sections to reflect a variety of types of classroom work; Family Message Journal entries comprised one section. Samples from this notebook were then used for formal evaluation purposes and as specific examples to discuss during family conferences.

The comparison of Kyle's messages at the beginning of the chapter illustrated that Family Message Journals reveal a wide range of information about a child's content-area and literacy learning that can be used to document growth and inform a teacher's instructional planning. In order to explore the usefulness of the journals as tools for evaluation, I analyzed and coded all of the case-study children's messages focusing on features of messages' rhetorical content (e.g., leads, degree of explanation, persuasiveness) and conventions (e.g., format, cohesion, spelling) because these are the two broad areas which reflect (in text) writers' awareness of their readers and of the nature of successful written communication. This analysis illuminated how children's writing changed over time with respect to content and conventions and resulted in an emergent framework for evaluating the first-grade writers' growth over the course of the year. Additionally, because one goal of the Family Message Journals was to use writing as a tool for learning across the curriculum, I also analyzed messages for evidence of learning about the topics studied in the classrooms.

From this multifaceted analysis of messages, I developed the following categories. Children's messages revealed their knowledge of the following:

1. appropriate content for a message
2. text-level conventions
3. sentence-level conventions
4. word-level conventions
5. topics studied

In the following paragraphs, I discuss how examples from the case-study children's Family Message Journals reflect growth of knowledge in these areas. Of course, all of the examples throughout this book can be examined through the lens of evaluation, and many readers will have already noted growth in each of the areas outlined. Also, it is important to point out that just as Kyle's examples reflect growth in multiple areas, so too do most of the children's entries. Looking at one facet of growth at a time is simply a convenience for discussion.

Appropriate Content for a Message

The most obvious indicator of growth in the content of children's messages is their length. All of the children began the year writing one sentence or less. By the end of the year, nearly all were writing messages of at least one page and, in most cases, several pages. There was growth in the quality of message content, as well. One aspect of this growth was audience awareness. For example, the first graders became increasingly adept at grabbing their readers' attention. Sara's message about wild animals begins with an attention-getting question:

> 3/2/97
> Dear Mom dad and Rosa
> would you like to be cept in a cage? well wild animals dos'n like to be in cages that's why ime asking you. can you name four wild animals I can name two lion and tiger Love Sara

Again indicating her awareness of her audience and of the dialogic nature of the message exchange, in another year-end message Sara answered a question her father had posed in his previous reply. He had asked if she thought her younger sister would like to visit the Children's Museum, as Sara's class had done on a field trip. Sara answered in a postscript to her message on a different topic:

> P.S. I do think Rosa will like it

Like Sara, most of the first graders began to answer families' questions in writing only toward the end of the school year, demonstrating their growing awareness of their roles in the written dialogue and their responsibility to keep up their end of the conversation and satisfy their readers' needs.

Another example of growth in the content of children's messages comes from comparing early and later requests for particular books from book club order forms that were regularly distributed in class. Early in the year, Maryanne simply began her messages: "I want to get . . . " or "Can I please get . . . ." But her later messages revealed awareness that her message would be more effective if she told her family *what* she was writing about first:

> January 10, 1997
> Dear Mommy
> I have a book ortor. these are the books Ied like ples. 101 dalamaicions krats creetures and little polar bear finds a frend.
> Love, Maryanne

Chapter 5 discussed requests for things like books, showing how the children developed increasingly sophisticated persuasive techniques to win approval for ideas and get what they wanted. This, too, was a sign of growth in audience awareness.

In the preceding journal entry, Maryanne's first sentence, which situates her message, shows a growing understanding of the nature of writing—it should be able to stand on its own, without the author present to explain. This knowledge was also evident in the children's developing skill at elaboration in their writing. Over time they grew better at telling everything necessary to fully communicate what they had learned. Consider a November message from Kyle which read simply: "The Indians planted corn," in comparison with a message written in March:

> 3/6/97
> Dear mom
> owls look wise B [but] the are not as smart as crows or blue Jays Before it hatchs a Baby owl has an egg Tooth The tooth is on it's Beak. The BaBy uses. The Tooth t crack The shell of the egg.

Kyle provides very complete information on how a baby owl gets out of its shell.

Another aspect of elaboration is the provision of evidence or reasoning to support one's ideas or assertions. The following message about a reptile presentation Kristen's class attended is a typical example of the first graders' growth in ability to support their assertions in writing:

> 3/20/97
> Dear Family,
> We saw a isebly [assembly] And got to see a frog And all kinds of snacse And we got to tuch soem Animalls I loved it. it was grate And We got to see a aligater And a trtle And we Liked it I wish you cud see the hole thing Becaus it was awsom that's why I liked it I Bet you wud to And the man was nise and youed love it And my favorite was the afrcen Bull Dog and the Boa cinstructer can not hear And it smells with it's nose Love Kristen P.S I Love you very much

Kristen explained the many reasons she thought the assembly was "awesome"—she got to see and touch many reptiles, and the man showing them was nice and had some interesting information to share, which Kristen relayed to her family. As in Maryanne's "I have a book ortor," by this point in the year Kristen also knew to begin with a sentence that contextualized the message for her family, explaining that the class had attended an assembly presentation.

Similarly, Sara learned to open with an indication of her message topic and then develop her message to share all she had learned:

> 6/2/97
> Dear Family
> We are talking about frogs we got a Weekly Reader about frogs and Scientists have discovered a frog it is littler than most frogs

and we learned about how they grow and about a poison dart
frog that is piosin and it has lite colors on it so the animals that
eat that kind of frog won't eat it and we leanded [learned] about
other frogs Love Sara

This message shows a great deal of growth from Sara's early messages,
which often jumped into sharing information, leaving her family confused
as to what the information was about. Also, her early messages usually did
not include such a full accounting of what she had learned.

A final example of how Family Message Journals can reflect
growth in children's awareness of appropriate message content comes
from Maryanne's journal:

> March 18, 1997
> Dear family I know Spring is comeing because pusywillows are
> evrywher we are growing some in out classroom. It is getting
> warmer evryday did you knowtiss? I remember we have flowers
> growing in our garden do you remember? And we are going to
> floreda very soon and scins we are going in the springtime and
> thats very soon and thats how I know
>> Love
>> Maryanne

This message demonstrates Maryanne's recognition that she should
provide evidence to back up her claim that spring is coming. Reflecting
thoughtful reasoning, she provides multiple pieces of evidence and also
speaks directly to her readers, asking questions which help to make her
voice come through clearly in her writing.

Text-Level Conventions

By comparing children's messages over the course of the school year, it
was easy to detect growth in text-level conventions such as genre and
format, as well as handwriting. One example of the first graders'
increasing facility with genre conventions is evidenced in their messages which were original stories. Compare two of Maryanne's stories,
written almost three months apart:

> December 21, 1996
> Ther once was a playn old show [shoe] who wanted too be spe-
> cial the show was naemed Joanna whent to the pant shope it
> jumped in too soum pant and ran back too the show shope Joanna
> talked to the auther [other] show's then a littel girl came by and
> buaut [bought] the show and Joanna had a awsam lighf

> March 6, 1997
> Last year Pickles the cute and little kitten was at the pet shop. the
> neighbors dog was looking in the window Pickles was scard she

un locked her cayg and juumed out and ran out the door climed up a tree. the dog barcked and barcked and finely gave up. Pickles climed down. Pickles ran to Pogos house. Pogo was Pickles identickal twin. back with the neighbor Brus the dog sliped out of his colar and went after the kittys. Soon he met up with them. Quickly the two cats ran home. When ther owners found them at the door they quickly let them in. they scureyed up the stairway and ran down the hall. ther sleepy roo [room] was behind the door. the door was clowsed scintc [since] they could not owpen it all by them selvs they hade to asck ther owner too owpen it, by meyowing. Ther owner owpened the door and Pogo and pickles saw Pixie and Pete on ther bed. Pixie and Pete wock [woke] up and welcomed them in, and all four kittens fell asleep with sweet dreams. The end

Whereas the reader does not know that the first story begins in a shoe store until the end, Maryanne's second story opens with an introduction to the setting, time, and main character. Both stories include the language of literature, the first beginning with "There once was," but the second story applies this language more consistently. Maryanne carefully chose words and phrases she might not use in everyday conversation but which one would find in a book, such as "scurried," "welcomed them in," and "all four kittens fell asleep with sweet dreams." Other first graders' stories also reflected growth in similar story conventions over the course of the year. For example, many moved from jumping into the plot without introducing the setting to using "Once upon a time" or "Once, in a forest, a long time ago" to situate readers and make their writing "sound like a story."

Maryanne's second story also reflects her expanding awareness of how to construct a story plot with a real problem to create tension and a satisfying resolution. She developed the plot more fully in the second example, describing what is happening and why. She also created internal consistency, explaining how the dog got free and how the kittens got the door open. The second story does not end until the kittens' problem is solved and we know what happens to them; the first one asks the reader to take a leap of faith, accepting that Joanna the shoe had an "awesome life."

Like Maryanne, other children also developed greater ability to weave complex story lines. Kristen's story, written in June, is a good example, reflecting many conventions of the fairy tale genre:

Ones upon a time there was a little man who needid a wife so he disided to make a ginger bread womon a few ours later she was doen he opened the oven then she poped out she ran thro the gate and out of the yard. Then she came to a farm She saw a horse

> The house [horse] smeled The ginger bread womon and she was
> she started to when the horse said do you won't to stay for lunch
> The ghinger bread womon saw soem farmers the farmers smeled
> the ginger bread womon geuss what the farmers said do you wan't
> to stay for lunch the ginger bread womon said no thank you the
> ginger Bread womon ceped [kept] running until she came to a
> lake with a swan in it the swan came to the side of the lake the
> side that the ginger bread womon was on the ginger Bread womon
> new if she swam she wood get soggy and brack [break] so the
> swan asked the ginger Bread womon if she cood get on her head
> when they were hafe [half] way threw the swan tost the ginger
> Bread womon up in the air But the ginger Bread womon landed
> on a rock in the mittle of the lake a egle swoped down and picked
> up the ginger Bread womon and ate it and that was the end of the
> ginger Bread womon.

This complex tale embodies the message that not one of the characters
the woman encounters (horse, farmers, and swan) is to be trusted, as is
often the case in such traditional stories, and it also incorporates humor
in the multiple interpretations of the question, "Do you want to stay for
lunch?" The woman's haste to get away suggests she understands this
invitation may mean that she *is* lunch! An unhappy ending also reflects
Kristen's sophisticated awareness of the genre—stories like this do not
always end with a "happily ever after," as the first graders' stories
always did at the start of the year.

Similar growth was observed in children's nonfiction writing.
Earlier, I discussed children's developing use of conventions of essay
writing, such as providing evidence for their statements, as in Kristen's
"reptile assembly" message, or organizing information to explain how
something happens, as in Kyle's "egg tooth" message.

Over time, children also became more adept at following conventions of letter form, as the examples throughout this book demonstrate.
Though some rarely included a date, most children began to do so
consistently by the second half of the year. The first graders also
regularly began to use a salutation at the beginning of their messages,
start a new line (sometimes even indenting the first line of the message
itself), and end with a closing. These are changes in the use of text-level
conventions that are easy for teachers and families to detect and track.

A final text-level convention that is important when communicating through print is handwriting. Children's handwriting varied somewhat from message to message, some messages appearing much neater
than others. This variation usually reflected how much they wrote and
how much time they had to work on their messages that day. Sometimes
messages on topics in which they were deeply interested were less neat

because the children were too involved to think about legibility as they furiously wrote ideas. Nevertheless, clear trends in handwriting were evident over time, as demonstrated by comparing any two of the same child's entries written even a month apart. Putting a September and a May or June message side by side revealed a striking contrast in all of the children's writing. Figure 7.3 shows Kristen's September message about a rainbow she had drawn:

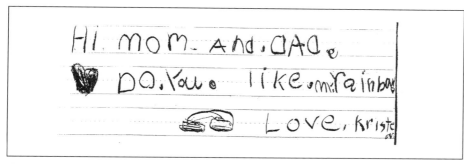

Figure 7.3. A message written by Kristen early in the school year.

And Figure 7.4 shows the first page of an early May message about the many scientific uses of trees:

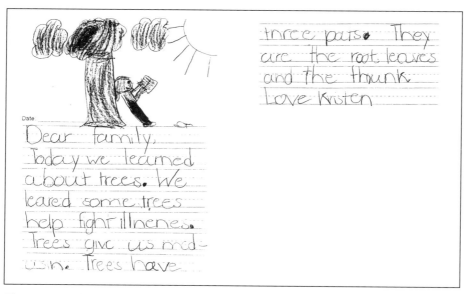

Figure 7.4. Kristen's May message about trees reflects growth in multiple aspects of handwriting ability.

Like Kristen, over the course of the year all of the first graders developed greater ability to form letters correctly, use proper spacing between letters and words, keep the size of their writing consistent within a message, keep their writing on the line, and start a new line when appropriate. Children's growth in the various aspects of hand-writing contributed to its legibility, an important factor when writing for an audience who will read one's messages on a daily basis.

Sentence-Level Conventions

Sentence-level conventions include the use of punctuation and of lexical links to create cohesion across sentences. When looking at the use of conventions, particularly sentence-level and word-level conventions, it is important to remember that the children did not formally edit their journal messages. Therefore, we cannot evaluate their ability to use the mechanics of writing based on Family Message Journals alone. Teachers would also want to assess how well children use these conventions in writing they have been asked to edit—work in which they have paid particular attention to mechanics. Nevertheless, as a bridge from informal to formal writing, composed for an audience that will rely on some degree of conventionality to understand the entries, Family Message Journals can provide insight into children's growing mastery of mechanics. Children were expected to reread each entry before bringing it home and were encouraged to add punctuation to help their readers.

Sara's Family Message Journal is typical in reflecting the first graders' growing ability to use the basics—periods, question marks, and exclamation marks—more consistently and correctly over time. At the beginning of the year, Sara rarely used punctuation, and when she did she placed a period between every word. By December she was able to place periods correctly most of the time, though she had to be reminded to add them, and she used capital letters properly sometimes, as in the following retelling of one chapter from *Frog and Toad Together* (Lobel, 1971):

> The first chapter was about toad. and He had lawts uv thing to do. Soa he roat a list. and it floo away latre. mi favrite one wus the gardin one. toad shoutid at the seeds.

Asking Sara to add punctuation to this originally unpunctuated message provided a clear picture of what she *could* do independently, as well as an indication that she still needed prodding to do it.

The first graders also gradually developed a more sophisticated use of punctuation such as commas and hyphens. In Kristen's year-end "gingerbread woman" story, when she came to the end of a line she twice used a hyphen to tie "ginger" on one line to "bread" on the next. However, she did not consistently follow conventions, as she also wrote the compound word as "ginger Bread" a number of times. This spotty use of sophisticated punctuation was typical—most of the first graders were just beginning to experiment with such advanced conventions at the end of the year. Nevertheless, this was a big improvement on Kristen's early messages in which, rather than using hyphens, she tried to squeeze a whole word onto a line even if it did not fit and was illegible. She never considered that a word might be continued on, or moved to, the next line (see, for example, her "rainbow" message in Figure 7.3).

Family Message Journals clearly documented the first graders' movement from no punctuation, to experimentation, to growing mastery of basic punctuation. When asked at the end of the year, the children were also able to explain *why* they used the punctuation marks they did. Having learned to punctuate in the context of authentic writing, they understood the specific function of each mark and the general purpose of punctuation in helping readers understand and appreciate the content of messages (Calkins, 1994; Wilde, 1992).

The first graders' Family Message Journals also reflect growth in the children's understanding of the need for cohesion across sentences (Halliday & Hasan, 1976; Kolln, 1999). Readers need to know how sentences and ideas are related, or else a message seems like a list of disconnected, rambling facts. Sara's "frog and toad" message is an example of the confusion caused by this lack of cohesion. "And it flew away later," referring to the list toad made for himself, is followed by "And my favorite one was the garden one." It is not clear what "one" refers to here, nor how this sentence relates to the previous sentence. A reader is left wondering whether Sara is referring to the list, to a different event in the same chapter, or to a different chapter.

Later in the year, Sara, like most of her classmates, grew far more adept at achieving cohesion throughout a message. This growth accompanied children's developing awareness of the need to elaborate on a topic. They gradually realized that a writer needs to *guide* readers to make sense of a message. Sara's message about dinosaurs guides her readers, helping them follow her train of thought by using lexical ties such as repetition of the word *dinosaurs* and pronouns which clearly refer to certain proper nouns:

> 3/13/97
> Dear Mom Dad and Rosa
> Did you know that their is a bigger dinosaur then T. rex? it's name
> is Carcharodontosaurus did you know their wusent any one
> airowned wen the dinosaurs wer alive? not even cave men their
> wer ol difirint cindse of dinosaurs their was tuiranasoris rex and
> T. rex and Carcharodontosaurus but I thingk their is a dinosaur
> named Pachecephylosaurus and their wer much more cindse of
> dinosaurs Love Sara

Sara structured her message to indicate that the first "it's" refers to
"Carcharodontosaurus," and when she changed the subject to the
absence of "cave men," she was careful in the next sentence to explicitly
mark that she was coming back to the subject of dinosaurs: "their wer ol
difirint cindse of dinosaurs." Earlier in the year she would typically
have written just "their wer ol difirint cindse," which would refer,
grammatically, to "cave men" and thereby confuse her readers, however briefly.

Like Sara, her classmates developed the ability to perceive when
they needed to make links explicit and to include information to make
their thinking transparent and avoid reader confusion. As this ability
developed, their messages became easier to read—it took less work to
figure out what they were referring to and what they meant.

Word-Level Conventions

At the word level, Family Message Journals were powerful evidence of
the first graders' growth in spelling, as well as a testament to the
wonderfully original reasoning evident in children's phonetic and
transitional spellings. At the beginning of the year, all of the children
were either prephonetic or semiphonetic spellers, writing only some of
the sounds in a word (Wilde, 1992). An early message written by Kristen
is a good example:

> 9/12/96
> I. want. to. learn. how. to. jemp. of. a. dving. BoD.

Kristen copied the first words of her message from the chalkboard but
had to invent spellings for the words in the second half. She represented
only some of the sounds in "diving" and "board" and, as is typical of
phonetic spellers, had trouble with the nasalized short vowel in "jump"
and omitted the second, silent "f" in *off*.

Looked at in their entirety, the first graders' messages demonstrate gradual movement toward consistent phonetic spelling, in which
all sounds in a word are represented as articulated. By March Kristen

had a store of sight words and relied on transitional spellings—those incorporating visual memory of ways she had seen certain sounds spelled with some phonetic spellings:

> 3/5/96
> Dear Famliy,
> We have been at school for 111 days. I have learned to read and spell And I leard to do Plusis Love Kristen

Kristen spelled "learned" correctly once, but as a typical phonetic speller, when she used it the second time she left out the difficult to discriminate "n." And while nearly all of the other words in this message are spelled correctly or by visual memory (e.g., "Famliy"), "plusis" is still phonetic.

Another example of the transitional spellings that were common by midyear is found in Sara's February message about the coming of spring, when she can "wride bicse and go to the playgrownd." Sara relied on her memory of various spelling patterns for the sounds she was trying to reproduce and came up with logical, if incorrect, hypotheses.

Children's growth in spelling was evident not only in their products—the messages—but also in the processes I observed them using to figure out spellings and in their growing attention to spelling, although content clearly remained their primary concern. Simply realizing that a word was not spelled correctly was a big step forward for many of the first graders. By watching as they wrote, I could see development over time as the children began to use spelling strategies, such as writing a word several ways to see what looked right or working out a problem with a peer. I also observed the growing use of spelling resources, such as referring to a familiar book about dinosaurs to help with the spelling of their names.

Topics Studied

As previously discussed in looking at how children learned to elaborate on the topics of their messages, we could also see clear evidence of *what* they had learned on those topics. Because Family Message Journals are used to record learning experiences and other activities which occur across the curriculum and the school day, teachers can use children's messages to assess what they recall and comprehend. Since messages recount information in the children's own words, they are a good indicator of what the children have truly understood and assimilated.

Throughout this book, we have seen evidence of children's learning in all of their messages. Any message can be used to assess the impact of a particular lesson or activity on children's thinking. The message highlighted in Figure 7.2 confirms that Kyle has learned a lot about automobile safety and feels it is quite important. Likewise, Kyle's "egg tooth" message and Sara's "frog" message, for example, reflect these first graders' growing knowledge.

Such messages recounting information learned can also be compared over time. For example, in early January, as part of a unit on dental health, Kyle participated in a lesson about baby teeth and their loss. Afterward, he wrote:

> Yo mom did you know that baby teeth are lesten [less than] a inch tol

In mid-March, after a lesson on dinosaurs, he wrote:

> 3/13/97
> Dear MoM and dad we are learning adout dinosaurs They are big my favrit valoserrapter, and Ducky u saurus, did you Know That carcharodontosaurus is higer than a T. rex? love kyle

The second message demonstrates that Kyle has recalled more information from the March activity, including various dinosaur names and information about dinosaur size in general and size relative to each other.

A message written by Maryanne about a unit on bats also indicates how much she has learned about bats' habits and habitats, interactions with people, and uses as a natural pest deterrent:

> March 10, 1997
> Dear Daddy
> I know that bats might bight you. Some peppel make bat houses because they want bats near by. bats need dark houms [homes]. Bats sleep during the day. bats might mouv into your adick if you have one. bats need dark houms. Bats sleep a lot. Some pepple put bats in the doorways of cavs so pepple and bats enemmys may not get in to bother them. thats all I know. Love, Maryanne

Maryanne's last sentence indicates that she has told everything she can remember, helping her teacher assess the extent of the information she has learned and can recall.

Another type of content learning which showed up in the children's Family Message Journals was their recall of stories they had read. Frequently, the first graders were asked to write messages retelling a story they had read independently. They were invited to finish the statement, "This story was about . . ." These messages gave the teachers a sense of children's understanding of the story's plot, characters, and theme or message, as well as a sense of how the children felt about the story. Examined over time, these messages also indicated growth in comprehension, recall, and appreciation. Consider the following set of retellings by Kyle. The first was written in November about a story called "Pet Wash" (de Paola, 1989):

> This story was about a pet, wash, and theawer lo's av [there were lots of] Pet's and PeoPle

This message briefly mentions the types of characters in the story but tells nothing about the plot or theme.

Another retelling by Kyle was written in January about a story entitled "On the Bus" (de Paola, 1989):

> This story was about eaveryone Geting on The Bus Max Got on the Bus Ead [Ed] sat in back and sat with Max and gave him sam Nas [some nuts] they wor freans [friends] and Carlos and Rod and he Had a new freaned love Kyle

This second retelling reflects considerable growth: most of the characters are included here by name, as is the setting (getting on the school bus in the morning) and the critical moment in the plot—when frighteningly big Ed sits down next to small Max, shares his nuts, and turns out to be not so bad after all. Though the message that people should not judge others by their appearance is not stated, Kyle does explain that Max and his friends Carlos and Rod (who also initially feared Ed) now have a new friend.

A third retelling, written by Kyle in mid-March and based on "Goblin Story" in *Little Bear's Visit* (Minarik, 1961), demonstrates further growth:

> This story was about a sily goblin who thot that his shoe was a moster and Juped [jumped] out of his shoe's and They ran after hem and juped in a tree he saw a cave and Thawt That There was a monster and he was scarde he had a brow hat and he had a beed and a green shirt and green shoes and he was white

This retelling shows progress not only in terms of length but also in terms of character description (added at the end) and awareness of the character's feelings and the motivation for his behavior. Kyle also includes his personal response to the goblin, calling him "silly," which reflects his understanding and appreciation of the humor in the story.

Of course, the ability to include in a message all that is recalled is somewhat dependent on a child's writing abilities, so assessment of content-area learning and reading comprehension must be integrated with assessment of writing skills and techniques. In any case, regardless of their length journal messages can help teachers understand what children have learned and what stood out for them most in a lesson or a text they have read.

Observing Children as They Write

Up to this point I have treated evaluation as product-focused by looking primarily at what the children's messages revealed both independently and as a collection over time. But teachers can also learn a great deal by observing while children write, gaining insight into the evolving *processes* they use to create their products. For example, as I observed over the course of the year, the first graders' abilities to attend to their writing, to get ideas down on paper quickly, and to use strategies to recall information they wanted to include in a message all changed strikingly. So, too, did their use of collaboration—they talked more about what they were writing, got ideas from one another as they composed, and used each other as resources for solving problems, such as spelling and punctuation questions. Their talk while writing was increasingly task-focused and was accompanied by fewer visits to the sharpened-pencil bin or the bathroom.

Observation can also reveal children's attitudes about writing and themselves as writers. These are important components of writing development—if children do not enjoy writing, or feel incapable of doing it well, it will be difficult for them to engage in message writing and to make progress over the course of the year. I found that by watching children's body language as they wrote, noting their reactions to the announcement that it was Family Message Journal time, and listening to what they said casually about themselves and their messages, I could detect considerable growth, especially among those who began the year as reluctant, self-doubting writers. These children came to feel better about their abilities and to enjoy writing, even if they could not stick with it as long as some of their more capable peers. By the end of October, though a few children still struggled to get anything legible down on paper, all expressed enjoyment of message writing, and the entire class protested vigorously when there was an occasional day without time for writing messages.

I observed the first-grade classroom for only part of one day each week. Teachers will be able to make more finely tuned observations of attitude than I could, since they know their students better and are in the classroom all the time.

Using Family Message Journals for Assessing Reading as Well as Writing

Although I did not explore Family Message Journals as a tool for formally assessing children's reading, Dina Carolan and Karen Wilensky use them in this capacity because the journals provide high-interest texts with familiar language that allows children to demonstrate their reading abilities.

Generally, once a week the teachers sit with each first grader individually and ask the child to read aloud his or her set of messages from the past week. They listen for "the child's ability to read the messages and replies, and for fluency and expression." They also ask the child to "identify names, other words, and punctuation marks by pointing, and to paraphrase the entries" to assess comprehension and encourage discussion of the writing. This takes only a few minutes, and while the teachers are noting information about the child's reading growth and needs, they can also note the kinds of progress in their written products discussed in this chapter.

Although she used to "try to check every child's message every day," Dina explained to me that if she "reads all of a child's messages once a week," staggering the days so that she is looking at only about five journals a day and then sitting with the five children individually to assess their reading, she can actually learn more about each one's progress, and the approach is more manageable.

The Role of Family Message Journals in Promoting and Assessing Learning

Of course, children's positive attitudes, their growing use of writing techniques and mechanics, and the content-area knowledge their messages displayed are not solely a result of writing in Family Message Journals. Natural cognitive and fine-motor development, as well as classroom discussions, activities, and direct instruction, certainly interacted with and contributed to their learning. So, too, did wide reading of texts modeling conventions and techniques of writing. Some children also had out-of-school experiences related to these areas of growth. And other types of writing sometimes occurred in the first-grade classrooms in addition to the Family Message Journals. Nevertheless, the journals contributed to children's learning by giving them a regular context in which to use writing to learn, a place to experiment with and practice techniques and conventions, and the responsibility for communicating with a real audience outside of the classroom.

Because Family Message Journals involve a particular type of writing, we must assess children's attitudes toward and abilities in writing by looking at a variety of writing experiences. As a collection of writing done over an entire school year, however, the Family Message Journals are a rich and varied source of ongoing evidence of learning, complementing other sources. These other sources should include other types of work the children do and also integrate the voices of all involved, including the children and their families.

Student Self-Evaluation

As noted earlier, one way to tap the perspectives of the first graders is through observing and listening as they participate in lessons related to Family Message Journals, write in their journals, and read and share families' replies. But children can also formally self-evaluate. Their self-evaluations can help to complete the picture of their abilities and attitudes related to writing. At the same time, and most important, self-evaluation encourages children to look back at and reflect on their work, helping them appreciate the progress they have made and set personal goals for improvement.

One reason the first-grade teachers like to keep all of the journal entries together in one folder is that this allows children to look back and reflect. Every three months or so they ask children to evaluate their messages by responding to one of the following prompts:

> I think I'm doing really well in . . .
>
> Have you noticed my . . . ?
>
> Have you noticed that I have gotten better at . . . ?

Using these prompts or similar ones, Dina says, children prove they "really know what they do well and what they need to improve at, and they can see their own progress—they notice the changes in their messages." Asking them to self-evaluate gives students the opportunity to use their self-awareness and reflective skills.

Another way to structure student self-evaluation would be to ask children to fill out a questionnaire like the following several times a year.

> FAMILY MESSAGE JOURNAL SELF-EVALUATION
> First, look over the messages you've written in your Family Message Journal. Think about what you wrote and how you wrote it. Then write about your messages:
> 1. I do a good job at Family Message Journals. You can tell because
> 2. I have gotten better at

3. I still need to work on
4. When it is time to write in my Family Message Journal, I feel
5. My favorite thing about Family Message Journals is
6. What I don't like about Family Message Journals is

As with Dina's and Karen's prompts, children need to be guided through the questionnaire, with the teacher initially modeling an array of possible answers, and they need plenty of time to look over their work carefully. Also, Dina and Karen have found that it is best to limit the messages they are considering to those written over a period of several months. Trying to look at the entire year's collection in June, for example, would probably overwhelm the first graders rather than spark thoughtful reflection.

Children can also be asked to select messages to put in their portfolios alongside the teacher's selections. Asking them to write a rationale for inclusion of their chosen entries is a good way to encourage reflection and tap children's sense of their strengths and areas needing improvement. Sometimes Dina and Karen include children's responses to their self-evaluation prompts along with a message or set of messages in the portfolio. Student self-evaluation is an important component of good instruction as well as assessment because it positions children as active learners, helping them focus on accomplishments and consciously work at weaknesses.

Family Evaluation

A final perspective contributing to evaluation of the Family Message Journals and of children's literacy and learning in general is that of families. As explained in Chapter 6, parents recognized that they could assess children's strengths and weaknesses and track their progress by looking at the first graders' messages individually and over time. In addition to these informal observations, families' evaluations can be sought systematically to complement teachers' perspectives.

When their students respond to self-evaluation prompts every few months, Dina and Karen ask families to reply, too. For example, when children write, "I think I'm doing really well in . . . ," parents are asked, "What do you think?" or "What have *you* noticed about my messages?"

Again, a questionnaire is a useful and more structured, though time-consuming, tool:

FAMILY MESSAGE JOURNAL EVALUATION—FAMILY SURVEY
Family Message Journals are one way to evaluate children's writing abilities and knowledge development, and to determine

their strengths, progress, and areas needing improvement. This helps me to plan instruction to meet the children's needs. Since you see the Family Message Journals daily, you probably have many insights into your child's work, too. Working together, we can help your child do his or her best in school. Please take a few minutes to fill out this questionnaire. I appreciate your input!

1. Do Family Message Journals help your child learn? How?
2. Do Family Message Journals help your child develop as a writer? How?
3. Do Family Message Journals help you assess your child's progress? How?
4. Look over the messages your child has written from September through December [or January through June]. Some things you *might* notice include: content and clarity, spelling, punctuation, format, and handwriting. What progress do you see?
5. What do you think your child still needs to work on?
6. Is there anything else you think I should know?

Because the replies to the self-evaluation prompts and the survey are open-ended, families can write as much or as little as they want, allowing them to provide input without overburdening them. It is important that families' perspectives not only be sought but also be clearly assigned value—in subsequent family conferences or in written progress reports, teachers must refer specifically to what families wrote. In fact, understanding families' perspectives helps Dina and Karen plan for conferences. We have to remember that families are too busy to provide a response or fill out a questionnaire that turns out to be busywork the teacher never considers seriously.

Keeping Evaluation in Perspective

Amid this discussion of evaluation, it is important to remember that the purpose of determining where children stand and what they have learned is not just to measure children's knowledge or ability. Rather, the primary purpose of evaluation should be to gather information that will help in planning appropriate instruction. Evaluation should be a teaching tool, not a sorting exercise.

Evaluating Family Message Journal entries aids in planning lessons that address children's needs. For example, Dina Carolan planned a lesson on using "P.S." when she saw children trying to tack information onto the end of their messages and then adding a second closing. Another series of lessons which grew out of early messages focused on audience awareness. Dina asked her first graders to think about the following: "What do you have to tell your family so they will understand?" Or, "What does your family need to know to make sense of this message?" She also modeled clear and less clear messages and discussed them with the children. Lessons on writing conventions grew out of Family Message Journal evaluation, too. For example, Dina observed that the children's only spelling strategy at the beginning of the year was to "sound it out," so she used several prewriting minilessons to develop alternate strategies such as trying to picture the word, using classroom resources such as the word wall and available books, and asking a friend for help. Messages also helped Dina understand what children had learned on a topic, suggesting which aspects of a content-area lesson might need review.

The Family Message Journal program itself also needs to be evaluated. Family input, along with children's perspectives and the teacher's observations, can help to suggest what is working and what needs modification. Over the years, Dina Carolan and Karen Wilensky have made modifications to their program, and they continue to do so in order to improve the program in general, iron out logistical wrinkles, and address the needs of each particular group of children,because the needs change yearly along with the children.

Evaluating Assumptions about Writing Instruction

As stated in Chapter 1, examining the writing children do in Family Message Journals can help us think incisively about writing instruction in general. My exploration of the journals revealed important insights related to how writing is taught and how children develop a sense of what writing is for. First, the success of Family Message Journals affirms the importance of writing for an audience beyond the classroom. Children developed an understanding of writing as purposeful, authentic communication. They were eager to write, and they were motivated to write clearly and to express their ideas fully and in an engaging manner because they were writing for an out-of-class audience.

Second, looking at Family Message Journal entries affirms the value of writing as an instrument of learning, thinking, and remembering across the curriculum. Entries reflected the use of writing as a tool and demonstrated to teachers and families that the first graders were using writing to reflect, recall, and relate ideas. Moreover, the children recognized these purposes for writing and talked about their appreciation for how writing could help them learn and remember.

Third, the Family Message Journals suggest that we must seriously consider teaching children to recognize, appreciate, and appropriate multiple genres and functions for writing. Form and function are inextricably linked; teaching the many functions of writing necessarily entails teaching genre (Cooper, 1999). Teacher assignment of topic and genre, and intervention through systematic instruction based on teachers' goals and children's demonstrated needs, helped the first graders try out many types of writing. These forms of writing are often never introduced to elementary school children, and yet students are expected to be familiar with them when they enter middle and high schools. My exploration of Family Message Journals suggests that first graders can begin to learn about and appreciate multiple genres, functions, and topics for writing that they might never have discovered or tried on their own. Many of these forms are used in daily life outside of school or in the study of particular subject areas. We underestimate young children if we assume they cannot be invited to explore these types of writing or that they will find them dull or uninspiring. At the same time, it is important to note that the first-grade teachers not only taught children new ways to structure and use writing, but they also provided opportunities, through the Family Message Journal, for children to exercise the knowledge and power they already possessed as writers.

Fourth, although teacher intervention in what and how children write is necessary to introduce and teach the variety of genres, purposes, and topics the first graders drew on in their Family Message Journals, this need not preclude student ownership of the written product. Self-selection, then, is not the sole route to ownership. Rather, authentic audiences and purposes appear to be crucial components. This finding challenges much standard writing process pedagogy, with its adherence to self-selection of topic, purpose, and genre.

Finally, by examining the first graders' Family Message Journals, observing as the program was enacted in the classroom, and interviewing the families, I found that we must overcome our cynicism and replace it with faith in families' willingness to be involved. The families of the children in Dina Carolan's and Karen Wilensky's first-grade classrooms were not all highly educated, socioeconomically privileged, comfortable with school, or competent with written English. Nevertheless, they committed themselves to replying to children's messages as best they could. Their replies demonstrated interest in the children's ideas, supported the children's efforts, and often provided high-quality instructional feedback. The success of Family Message Journals suggests that we must reassess our typically low expectations for family involvement in children's school learning and think about how our invitations to families can be structured to make their involvement manageable and to capitalize on their willingness to help their children. If we are truly committed to family involvement, we may also need to broaden our views of families' roles and of inservice education. Teachers may learn from and *with* families, and families may play an important role in contributing to school curriculum and instruction (Moll, 1992).

It is my hope that this book will not only encourage other teachers to try to genuinely involve families in children's school learning and take seriously the potential benefits, but that it will also spur reflection on how we teach writing in general. Considering how Family Message Journals worked in two first-grade classrooms stimulates careful, critical thought about what "ownership" means and about how we might balance student choice and teacher direction in writing instruction. This study of Family Message Journals suggests that elementary school curricula and instruction might best be structured around some guiding questions:

- Are children consistently engaged in writing for real readers and reasons?
- Does the writing involve learning for both the writer and the audience?
- Are teachers scaffolding the process through systematic instruction that requires students to try new purposes, forms, and functions and to write with an awareness of their audience?

Dina and Karen have provided us with a model of classrooms in which these questions can be answered in the affirmative, helping to further our understanding of what works in elementary writing instruction.

Works Cited

Aldis, D. (1968). When. In S. C. Gross (Ed.), *Every child's book of verse*. New York: Franklin Watts.

Applebee, A. N., & Langer, J. A. (1983). Instructional scaffolding: Reading and writing as natural language activities. *Language Arts, 60*, 168–175.

Atwell, N. (1987). *In the middle: Writing, reading and learning with adolescents.* Upper Montclair, NJ: Boynton/Cook.

Atwell, N. (Ed.). (1990). *Coming to know: Writing to learn in the intermediate grades.* Portsmouth, NH: Heinemann.

Avery, C. S. (1987). First grade thinkers becoming literate. *Language Arts, 64*, 611–618.

Baumann, J. F., & Thomas, D. (1997). "If you can pass Momma's tests then she knows you're getting your education": A case study of support for literacy learning within an African American family. *The Reading Teacher, 51*, 108–120.

Bereiter, C., & Scardamalia, M. (1987). *The psychology of written composition.* Hillsdale, NJ: Erlbaum.

Bissex, G. (1980). *Gnys at Wrk: A child learns to write and read.* Cambridge, MA: Harvard University Press.

Bomer, R. (1998). Transactional heat and light: More explicit literacy learning. *Language Arts, 76*, 11–18.

Britton, J. (1970). *Language and learning.* London: Allen Lane.

Britton, J., Burgess, T., Martin, N., McLeod, A., & Rosen, H. (1975). *The development of writing abilities (11–18).* London: Macmillan Educational Books.

Bulla, C. R. (1989). *Singing Sam.* New York: Random House.

Cairney, T. H., & Munsie, L. (1995). *Beyond tokenism: Parents as partners in literacy.* Portsmouth, NH: Heinemann.

Calkins, L. M. (1986). *The art of teaching writing.* Portsmouth, NH: Heinemann.

Calkins, L. M. (1994). *The art of teaching writing* (New ed.). Portsmouth, NH: Heinemann.

Cambourne, B. (1988). *The whole story: Natural learning and the acquisition of literacy in the classroom.* Auckland, New Zealand: Ashton Scholastic.

Cazden, C. B. (1988). *Classroom discourse: The language of teaching and learning.* Portsmouth, NH: Heinemann.

Chapman, M. (1995). The sociocognitive construction of written genres in first grade. *Research in the Teaching of English, 29*, 164–192.

Christie, F. (1985). Language and schooling. In S. Tchudi (Ed.), *Language, schooling and society* (pp. 21–40). Upper Montclair, NJ: Boynton/Cook.

Christie, F. (1986). Writing in schools: Generic structures as ways of meaning. In B. Couture (Ed.), *Functional approaches to writing: Research perspectives* (pp. 22–39). London: Pinter.

Clay, M. (1975). *What did I write?* Exeter, NH: Heinemann Educational Books.

Cooper, C. R. (1999). What we know about genres, and how it can help us assign and evaluate writing. In C. R. Cooper & L. Odell (Eds.), *Evaluating writing: The role of teachers' knowledge about text, learning, and culture* (pp. 23–52). Urbana, IL: National Council of Teachers of English.

Dauber, S., & Epstein, J. (1993). Parents' attitudes and practices of involvement in inner-city elementary and middle schools. In N. Chavkin (Ed.), *Families and schools in a pluralistic society* (pp. 53–71). Albany: SUNY Press.

Delgado-Gaitan, C. (1990). *Literacy for empowerment: The role of parents in children's education.* New York: Falmer Press.

de Paola, T. (1989). *Grab that dog!* Lexington, MA: D.C. Heath.

Dudley-Marling, C. (1997). If students *own* their learning, what do teachers do? In B. M. Power, J. D. Wilhelm, & K. Chandler (Eds.), *Reading Stephen King: Issues of censorship, student choice, and popular literature* (pp. 73–82). Urbana, IL: National Council of Teachers of English.

Edelsky, C., Altwerger, B., & Flores, B. (1991). *Whole language: What's the difference?* Portsmouth, NH: Heinemann.

Emig, J. (1977). Writing as a mode of learning. *College Composition and Communication, 28,* 122–128.

Epstein, J. L. (1986). Parents' reactions to teacher practices of parent involvement. *Elementary School Journal, 86,* 277–294.

Epstein, J. L. (1991). Effects on student achievement of teachers' practices of parent involvement. In J. B. Silvern (Ed.), *Literacy through family, community, and school interaction*: Vol. 5. *Advances in reading/language research* (pp. 261–276). Greenwich, CT: JAI Press.

Epstein, J. L., & Dauber, S. L. (1991). School programs and teacher practices of parent involvement in inner-city elementary and middle schools. *Elementary School Journal, 91,* 289–305.

Fact and fiction. (1997 December/1998 January). *Reading Today,* p. 7.

Frank, L. A. (1992). Writing to be read: Young writers' ability to demonstrate audience awareness when evaluated by their readers. *Research in the Teaching of English, 26,* 277–298.

Fulwiler, T. (1982). The personal connection: Journal writing across the curriculum. In T. Fulwiler & A. Young (Eds.), *Language connections: Writing and reading across the curriculum* (pp. 15–31). Urbana, IL: National Council of Teachers of English.

Fulwiler, T. (1987). *The journal book.* Portsmouth, NH: Heinemann.

Glaser, B. G., & Strauss, A. L. (1967). *The discovery of grounded theory: Strategies for qualitative research.* Chicago: Aldine.

Graves, D. H. (1983). *Writing: Teachers and children at work.* Portsmouth, NH: Heinemann Educational Books.

Guba, E., & Lincoln, Y. (1981). *Effective evaluation.* London: Jossey-Bass.

Hall, N. (1998). Real literacy in a school setting: Five-year-olds take on the world. *The Reading Teacher, 52,* 8–17.

Halliday, M. A. K. (1975). *Learning how to mean: Explorations in the development of language.* London: Edward Arnold.

Halliday, M. A. K., & Hasan, R. K. (1976). *Cohesion in English.* London: Longman.

Hancock, M. R. (1993). Exploring and extending personal response through literature journals. *The Reading Teacher, 46,* 466–474.

Harste, J. C., Woodward, V. A., & Burke, C. L. (1984). *Language stories and literacy lessons.* Portsmouth, NH: Heinemann.

Hoover-Dempsey, K. V., & Sandler, H. M. (1995). Parental involvement in children's education: Why does it make a difference? *Teachers College Record, 97,* 310–331.

Hoover-Dempsey, K. V., & Sandler, H. M. (1997). Why do parents become involved in their children's education? *Review of Educational Research, 67,* 3–42.

Hopkins, L. B. (1990). *Good books, good times!* New York: Harper & Row.

King, M., & Rentel, V. (1979). Toward a theory of early writing development. *Research in the Teaching of English, 13,* 243–253.

Kolln, M. (1999). Cohesion and coherence. In C. R. Cooper & L. Odell (Eds.), *Evaluating writing: The role of teachers' knowledge about text, learning, and culture* (pp. 93–113). Urbana, IL: National Council of Teachers of English.

Kreeft, J. (1984). Dialogue writing—Bridge from talk to essay writing. *Language Arts, 61,* 141–150.

Langer, J. A. (1986). *Children reading and writing: Structures and strategies.* Norwood, NJ: Ablex.

Langer, J. A., & Applebee, A. N. (1986). Reading and writing instruction: Toward a theory of teaching and learning. *Review of Research in Education, 13,* 171–194.

Lionni, L. (1994). *An extraordinary egg.* New York: Knopf.

Lobel, A. (1971). *Frog and toad together.* New York: HarperFestival.

Martin, B., & Archambault, J. (1989). *Chicka chicka boom boom.* New York: Simon & Schuster.

Martin, N., D'Arcy, P., Newton, B., & Parker, R. (1976). *Writing and learning across the curriculum, 11–16.* London: Ward Lock.

Mayher, J., & Lester, N. (1983). Putting learning first in writing to learn. *Language Arts, 60,* 717–721.

Milz, V. (1985). First graders' uses for writing. In A. Jaggar & M. T. Smith-Burke (Eds.), *Observing the language learner* (pp. 173–189). Newark, DE: International Reading Association/Urbana, IL: National Council of Teachers of English.

Minarik, E. H. (1961). *Little bear's visit.* New York: Harper.

Moll, L. (1992). Bilingual classroom studies and community analysis: Some recent trends. *Educational Researcher, 21,* 20–24.

Mulhern, M. M. (1997). Doing his own thing: A Mexican-American kindergartner becomes literate at home and school. *Language Arts, 74,* 468–476.

Neuman, S. B., & Roskos, K. (1990). Play, print, and purpose: Enriching play environments for literacy development. *The Reading Teacher, 44,* 214–221.

Ninio, A., & Bruner, J. (1978). The achievement and antecedents of labelling. *Journal of Child Language, 5,* 1–15.

Pappas, C. C., & Pettegrew, B. S. (1998). The role of genre in the psycholinguistic guessing game of reading. *Language Arts, 75,* 36–44.

Paratore, J. R., Melzi, G., & Krol-Sinclair, B. (1999). *What should we expect of family literacy?* Newark, DE: International Reading Association/Chicago: National Reading Conference.

Quint, S. (1994). *Schooling homeless children: A working model for America's public schools.* New York: Teachers College Press.

Ratner, N., & Bruner, J. (1978). Games, social exchange and the acquisition of language. *Journal of Child Language, 5,* 391–401.

Ridlon, M. (1969). *That was summer.* Chicago: Follett.

Rogoff, B., & Gardner, W. (1984). Adult guidance of cognitive development. In B. Rogoff & J. Lave (Eds.), *Everyday cognition: Its development in social context* (pp. 95–116). Cambridge, MA: Harvard University Press.

Rosenholtz, S. (1989). *Teachers' workplace: The social organization of schools.* New York: Longman.

Routman, R. (1991). *Invitations: Changing as teachers and learners K–12.* Portsmouth, NH: Heinemann.

Ryder, P. M., Vander Lei, E., & Roen, D. H. (1999). Audience considerations for evaluating writing. In C. R. Cooper & L. Odell (Eds.), *Evaluating writing: The role of teachers' knowledge about text, learning, and culture* (pp. 53–71). Urbana, IL: National Council of Teachers of English.

Schleppegrell, M. J. (1998). Grammar as resource: Writing a description. *Research in the Teaching of English, 32,* 182–211.

Shockley, B., Michalove, B., & Allen, J. (1995). *Engaging families: Connecting home and school literacy communities.* Portsmouth, NH: Heinemann.

Taylor, D., & Dorsey-Gaines, C. (1988). *Growing up literate: Learning from inner-city families.* Portsmouth, NH: Heinemann.

Temple, C., Nathan, R., Burris, N., & Temple, F. (1988). *The beginnings of writing* (2nd ed.). Boston: Allyn & Bacon.

Vygotsky, L. S. (1978). *Mind in society: The development of higher psychological processes* (M. Cole, V. John-Steiner, S. Scribner, & E. Souberman, Eds.). Cambridge, MA: Harvard University Press.

Walsh, E. S. (1989). *Mouse paint.* San Diego: Harcourt Brace Jovanovich.

Watson, K., & Young, B. (1986). Discourse for learning in the classroom. *Language Arts, 63,* 126–133.

White, E. B. (1952). *Charlotte's web.* New York: Harper & Row.

Wilde, S. (1992). *You kan red this! Spelling and punctuation for whole language classrooms K–6.* Portsmouth, NH: Heinemann.

Wollman-Bonilla, J. E. (1989). Reading journals: Invitations to participate in literature. *The Reading Teacher, 43,* 112–120.

Wollman-Bonilla, J. E. (1991). *Response journals: Inviting students to think and write about literature.* New York: Scholastic.

Wollman-Bonilla, J. E., & Werchadlo, B. (1995). Literature response journals in a first-grade classroom. *Language Arts, 72,* 562–570.

Wollman-Bonilla, J. E., & Werchadlo, B. (1999). Teacher and peer roles in scaffolding first-graders' responses to literature. *The Reading Teacher, 52,* 598–608.

Wood, D., Bruner, J., & Ross, G. (1976). The role of tutoring in problem solving. *Journal of Child Psychology and Psychiatry, 17,* 89–100.

Author

A former elementary school teacher, **Julie Wollman-Bonilla** now teaches at Rhode Island College as a member of the Department of Elementary Education and the faculty of the Rhode Island College and University of Rhode Island joint Doctoral Program in Education. She works with undergraduate, masters, and doctoral students to help make schools better places for children and teachers to learn and grow. She is especially interested in language and literacy learning, writing and talk as tools for learning, sociocultural differences in discourse styles, and reforming pedagogy to include a commitment to social equity, providing all children with opportunities to achieve academic excellence. Affirming family backgrounds and knowledge and involving families as partners in children's school learning are important facets of such reform. Julie has written a number of articles and a book, titled *Response Journals: Inviting Students to Think and Write about Literature.*

This book was typeset in Palatino and Helvetica.
Typefaces used on the cover were Adobe Rotis Sans and Serif.
The book was printed by IPC Communication Services.